ENGLISH
SILVER
HALL-MARKS

Including the Marks of Origin on
SCOTTISH & IRISH SILVER PLATE
GOLD, PLATINUM & SHEFFIELD PLATE

With 300 of the more important
MAKERS MARKS FROM 1697–1900

edited by

Judith Banister

with lists of
English, Scottish and Irish
Hall-marks and Makers' Marks
from Circa 1554

LONDON
W. FOULSHAM & Co. Ltd.
NEW YORK   TORONTO   CAPE TOWN   SYDNEY

W. FOULSHAM & CO. LTD.,

Yeovil Road, Slough, Berks., England

ISBN 0-572-01181-4

© Copyright Design and Layout 1970
New Edition 1990
BELASCO

Printed in Great Britain by
St Edmundsbury Press Ltd.,
Bury St Edmunds, Suffolk

CONTENTS

ACKNOWLEDGEMENTS

The Publishers extend their thanks to the Masters of the Assay Offices of Dublin, Sheffield and Birmingham for the advice, guidance and material for reproduction which they were kind enough to supply.

In particular sincere thanks are extended to the Goldsmiths Company for the continuance support and assistance which they gave and for the right to reproduce the majority of Makers' marks from their records.

Also Acknowledged is the material reprinted from Goldsmiths & Their Marks by Sir Charles Jackson, Dover Publications, New York through whom permissions were obtained.

PREFACE

The intention underlying the publication of this Pocket Identification Guide has been to provide, for Collectors and Dealers alike, a portable reference source to the Assay Office Marks *and* more important Makers' Marks found on British silver and gold. The marks on platinum, as well as those on the most commonly encountered Sheffield plate, are also included.

In the tables containing the Assay Office Marks, it will be seen that each cycle has been contained in one box and that to the outside edge of each box an additional panel has been added. This layout was chosen to allow for the inclusion in the panels of an enlarged Assay Office Symbol, Date Letter and gold quality marks which we hope will provide for quicker visual location when "flipping through" the pages. This will be of value not only to those who do know something of hall-marking but also to those new collectors who know nothing of the devices adopted by the various Assay Offices. It is assumed that these Collectors will carefully read the Introduction but for them we would explain that having located the *style* of town mark and date letter in the outside panel all of the remaining marks on the piece in question must be checked against those reproduced in the box. This should confirm that the right period has been located and provide a date of Assay against the relevant date letter.

During the earliest working periods of some of the Assay Offices there is little consistency in the design of marks applied to silver. They change so frequently in the cycle boxes that it has been impossible to include anything very worthwhile in the exterior panels. For consistency, however, we have included the design that seems to be most representative of those in the boxes and hope that they will be of some value.

Finally, attention is drawn to the details of monarchs in each panel. These are included to show which of the sovereigns were reigning during each cycle. Where only one name is given, it can be taken that throughout that period there was no accession to the throne. Where there is a change of rule during the cycle, both monarchs and the date of accession are given.

The Makers' Marks found in the third section of the book are in the main of those whose work was done in London; though obviously we have included the most important makers from Birmingham, Dublin, Edinburgh and Sheffield. We have confined our coverage of them to the period 1697 to 1900 which we felt represented the period from which most antique silver is currently available. Obviously to include every silver maker of that period is out of the question in a book of this length and we therefore compiled a list of renowned or prolific silver makers and illustrated those of their marks which would ensure the identification of all of their work. Our reference source has been the Official records held by the Goldsmiths' Company in London whose permission and kind assistance we had in being allowed to photograph the marks entered by the London makers in the record books. For this reason we can reasonably claim that the section on Makers' Marks is one of the most accurate records available.

The only qualifying factor we would wish to place on the above statement is that though every mark represents an accurate impression of that entered in the record books, they are not necessarily proportionally accurate one to another. We have had to enlarge each mark for ease of identification but because of the great variety in their sizes and the standard width of our page, have been unable to achieve a standard degree of magnification.

Introduction

SILVER HALL-MARKS

Hall-marks are the authenticating marks struck on all modern and most old English, Scottish and Irish silver and gold. Since 1st January 1975 it has been necessary by law to include them on platinum also. They are official marks, applied only after testing that the standard, or quality, of the metal is right, but the term has also come to embrace the maker's mark. The hall-marking system in Britain has a long history, and it can claim to be the oldest form of consumer protection in the country.

In medieval England, regulation of the goldsmith's craft (the term goldsmith was formerly used without distinction for gold- and silver-smith) was in the hands of the London Goldsmiths' Company. Scotland has never been under their jurisdiction, though after the Act of Union, duties and other London-made laws were applied there. Dublin, likewise, has its own Company, to which Charles I granted a Charter in 1637; in Ireland there was no duty on silver until 1730, and the King's head duty mark there, did not appear until 1807.

The earliest statute concerning gold and silver is that of 1238 A.D., when the standards of fineness were laid down, but the true beginning of hall-marking dates from 1300 A.D., when it was decreed that no piece of silver "was to depart out of the hands of the workers" until it had been assayed (or tested) and marked with the leopard's head. The standard of silver was to be sterling, or 92·5 per cent. pure, which was the same standard as the coinage. At the same time, the "Guardians of the Craft" were instructed to go out among the workers to make sure that the law was enforced, and it was further enacted that "in all good towns of England where there are goldsmiths" the same should apply, and that one of their number should go to London "to seek their sure touch."

The Maker's Mark

In order to supervise the craft, it was obvious that some way had to be found to identify the maker of substandard wares,

7

and so in 1363 it was commanded that each Master Goldsmith should have his own mark, which had to be registered. In the past, the maker's mark took a variety of forms. Sometimes it was merely a symbol, perhaps his shop sign, or a rebus or pun on his name. Later, initials, often associated with one or more symbols or devices, became common. In 1696, with the introduction of the new higher Britannia Standard, all makers had to re-register their marks, and a completely new style was ordered – the use of the first two letters of the surname. In 1720, when the old sterling standard was restored, so were the old-style marks. Indeed, some makers were using marks of different styles at the same time, so in 1739 all were ordered to re-register with new marks, and from then on most marks took the form of initials of forename and surname, with only an occasional additional symbol such as a crown or a mullet.

The Date Letter

Towards the end of the 15th century, continued complaints about substandard wares resulted in a ruling that the "Keeper of the Touch" – in fact, the Assay Master – should be responsible for maintaining the standard. Probably that led to the date letter system, devised to ascertain the year of assay (and so to trace offending maker and assay-master as well) but by a happy chance also the silver collector's invaluable guide. The first full cycle of date letters in London started with A in 1478, and continued in 20-year cycles (omitting J, and from V to Z) without a break until 1696, when a new series commenced with the new Britannia standard. Since then, each new cycle, differentiated by changing styles of letter and/or shields, has been unbroken.

Outside London, both the length of each cycle and the year of commencement varies considerably, and it is advisable to consult the tables. In addition, slight confusion sometimes arises because assay offices change the year-letter at different times of the year – London changes in May, for instance, Birmingham and Sheffield in June, and Edinburgh in October.

The Leopard's Head

From early documents, it appears that the leopard's head, which was crowned until 1821, was the standard mark, but from 1544, when the lion passant gardant was added to the hall-marks, it became more accurately the authoritative mark of the Goldsmiths' Company, and today it remains as the London town mark. As the Company's mark of authority, it was used by several of the provincial assay offices in addition to their own town mark. In York and Newcastle it was used until those offices were closed in 1857 and 1883 respectively. In Chester it was used until 1838, in Exter until 1777, and it also appeared on the few known pieces of Bristol silver made about 1720-1760. Neither Birmingham nor Sheffield, understandably, used it, and it was seldom struck elsewhere, though various forms of leopard's head, usually debased, were used in East Anglia, in Shrewsbury and even in Jamaica. In 1821, for some unspecified reason, it was deprived of its crown.

The Lion Passant

Sometimes called the sterling mark, the lion passant gardant made its first appearance in 1544, at a period when the coinage, normally of sterling silver, was much debased. It was perhaps struck by the Goldsmiths' Company as an indication that their hall-marked wares were sterling, even if the coinage were not. In 1720 its use was extended to all the existing provincial English assay offices, and it was also adopted at Sheffield and Birmingham when they opened in 1773. In Chester, York and Sheffield the lion passant has always been *gardant*, that is, looking over its shoulder, but elsewhere it changed to being merely *passant* (looking ahead) in London in 1821, in Exeter in 1837, in Newcastle in 1846 and in Birmingham in 1875.

The Britannia Standard

In 1696, so extensive had become the melting and clipping of coinage that the silversmiths were forbidden to use the sterling standard for their wares, but had to use a new higher standard, 95·8 per cent. pure, or another 8 dwts. of silver to the pound troy. New hall-marks were ordered, the "figure of a woman commonly called Britannia" and the lion's head erased (torn off at the neck) replacing the lion passant and the leopard's head crowned. As noted above, a new series of date letters began in March 1697, and makers had to register new marks.

Since the Britannia standard silver was more expensive, the silversmiths began to clamour for the restoration of sterling, though some actually lodged a counter-petition to retain the higher standard, because of advantages in its working (it being softer) and on account of the export trade with Europe. Their pleas were acknowledged by the permission to retain the higher standard alongside sterling when the old standard was restored on June 1, 1720.

The Duty Mark

The price of restoration of sterling in 1720 was a duty of 6d. an ounce on wrought plate. This resulted in the practice known as "duty-dodging" by which some silversmiths avoided paying duty by incorporating pieces of plate bearing hall-marks into a new piece. The duty was removed in 1758, only to be re-imposed, at the same rate, in 1784. Payment of duty was, as before, exacted at the time of assay, but from 1784 until its abolition in 1890, the duty paid was recorded by another hall-mark, the sovereign's head mark. At first, from December 1, 1784, until May 1786, the king's head was incuse, but after that it appeared in cameo. The profiles of George III, George IV and William IV face to the right, the head of Queen Victoria to the left. The duty mark was also struck in Edinburgh from 1784 onwards, in Glasgow from 1819, and in Dublin from 1807. Curiously, some assay offices did not change the punch on the death of the sovereign, and William IV's head sometimes appears on Victorian silver made in Chester, Edinburgh, Glasgow, Newcastle, Sheffield and York as late as 1840 or 1841.

The Duty Drawback Mark, an incuse figure of Britannia standing, is almost certainly the rarest of all hall-marks. It was used for only eight months, from 1st December 1784 until July 1785, on plate exported from England. Being struck after the piece was polished and finished, it was liable to damage it, and was therefore withdrawn, silversmiths simply claiming drawback of duty against shipping notes or invoices.

Outside London

Many of the ancient ordinances and other documents mention goldsmiths outside London, and from time to time various towns have been named as Assay Towns and as Mint Towns. A few survived into the 18th century, and even into the 19th century, as assay towns – Chester, Norwich, Newcastle, Exeter and York, and, apparently, Bristol. For the rest, the wear and tear of the years, changing taste and the consignment of silver to the melting-pot for one reason or another has made the history of the provincial silversmiths of Britain both difficult to unravel and wholly absorbing. Considerable research has brought credible attribution of dozens of different marks to minor centres, and certain identification of many others, such as Barnstaple, Hull, Kings Lynn, Leeds, Plymouth, Taunton, Truro and so on.

The enforcement of the higher Britannia Standard appears to have put an end to one or two of the last centres of silversmithing that survived into the late 17th century. Indeed, the Act of 1696 actually completely ignored even the major provincial centres, and it was not until 1700 that the position was rectified so far as Chester, York, Norwich and Exeter were concerned, and even then Newcastle, a thriving centre of silversmithing right through the 18th century, was ignored until 1701.

Until 1700, only York and, to a lesser degree, Norwich, had any system of date letters, and by then both these towns were almost dormant. Exeter, Newcastle and Chester all continued to be active throughout the 18th century, using as their town marks a triple castle, three keeps and the Arms of the City of Chester respectively.

By the middle of the 18th century, both Birmingham and Sheffield were fast becoming large manufacturing centres for the trade, and largely through the efforts of Matthew Boulton, the Birmingham industrialist, despite the opposition of the London Goldsmiths' Company, an Act of Parliament set up the Birmingham and Sheffield Assay Offices in 1773, Birmingham taking the anchor as its mark, and Sheffield the crown.

Scotland

In 1457 A.D., James II of Scotland proclaimed a standard of 11 ozs. per lb. troy (i.e. 12 ozs.) for wrought silver. At the same time, the practice of striking a Deacon's (or Warden's) mark alongside that of the maker was instituted. In Edinburgh, the town mark, a triple-towered castle, was used from 1485 onwards, but it was 1681 before a date letter system was adopted. Then, too, an Assay Master's mark was substituted for that of the Deacon, until 1759, when it was replaced by the thistle standard mark.

Scotland was not subject to the Britannia Standard, but in 1720, when sterling was restored in England, the standard of silver was raised in Scotland to conform to the English sterling, 11 ozs. 2 dwts. pure per lb. troy, and the 6d. an ounce duty was also imposed.

In 1586, the Edinburgh Goldsmiths had been granted jurisdiction over the craft throughout Scotland, and that was reaffirmed in 1686, at which time there were goldsmiths recorded as working in Glasgow, Aberdeen, Perth, Inverness, Ayr, Banff and Montrose.

Considerable research has been done in recent years on the Scottish craftsmen outside Edinburgh. Glasgow had its own Incorporation of Hammermen by 1536, and in 1681 they too adopted a date letter system. It fell into disuse in the early 18th century, the letters S (perhaps for Sterling or for Scottish), O and E being much used, together with the town mark, a tree with a bird and bell, and a fish below. Glasgow's industrial growth resulted in the formation, in 1819, of an official Assay Office there, and the lion rampant was chosen as the standard mark. The sovereign's head duty mark was also struck, and in 1914 the thistle standard mark was added. The Glasgow Assay Office, which had been running at a loss for some years, was closed in 1964.

Until the rise of Glasgow, Aberdeen was probably the most important trading centre in Scotland outside Edinburgh, and from about 1600 onwards, various marks were used by the silversmiths, usually in the form of the letters AB, ABD or a contracted symbol, with a single or a three castle mark, very like that used in Newcastle. Aberdeen was actually divided into two burghs, Old Aberdeen, where a pike's head mark is associated with one Colline Allen about 1740/1760, and New Aberdeen, where most of the craftsmen worked.

At Banff, where silver was made from about 1680 to 1830, various versions of the name, from B to BANF were struck. At Dundee a pot-of-lilies appeared on silver from about 1625 to 1810, a device based on the town arms, and at Perth one of several marks used during the long history of silversmithing there was the lion and banner of St. John, though during the 18th century the mark changed to a double-headed eagle, the modern town symbol, which was used until about 1850. Inverness boasted silversmiths for some two centuries, from about 1640 to as late as 1880, a dromedary mark sometimes being used alongside the more usual INS abbreviation. Montrose naturally found itself with a rose mark, seen between about 1650 and 1820, at Arbroath there was a portcullis mark taken from the burgh seal, and at Greenock a "green oak" used from about 1760 to 1840 provided a punning mark much like the T over a tun of Taunton. At Wick and Tain the brief names were usually struck in full, Elgin was contracted to Eln or Elg, and used with a mother and child device said to have been based on the story of a widow who took refuge there in 1745. A tall fort mark has been attributed to Forres, a cross to St. Andrews, and another portcullis mark, with S at the base, to Stirling. Possibly PH stands for Peterhead, where a key mark may also have been used, but much work still remains to be done, not only in identifying town marks but in establishing where some of the itinerant craftsmen worked.

Ireland

Of all the gold and silversmiths in Britain, Ireland's have undoubtedly the longest unbroken history, dating back to the Bronze Age craftsmen. In the Middle Ages, the Dublin goldsmiths were a substantial guild, and in 1555 they were granted a Charter, which was followed by a Royal Charter in 1637. This prescribed the sterling standard, with the harp crowned as the standard mark, superseding a previous, but apparently unenforced, lion, harp and castle. In 1638 a date letter system began, but the series used and even the time each letter was used was somewhat haphazard, and in 1730, when a duty of 6d. an ounce was imposed and the duty paid indicated by a figure of Hibernia, often the date letter was omitted altogether. The Hibernia mark somewhat resembles the Britannia on English silver (as in Scotland, there was no era of Britannia silver in Ireland). Officially, it was struck as a tax "for the encouragement of tillage", but in 1806 Irish silver was struck with the king's head duty mark as well, so that the Hibernia tended to become the Dublin Assay Office mark.

makers mark   Britannia mark   standard mark   date letter

There are very full lists of makers registered with the Dublin Goldsmiths' Company, so that identification of most makers' marks from 1637 onwards is possible. From 1784 onwards, many provincial Irish silversmiths were also registered at

Dublin, and not a few names are recorded in the local records of Cork, Youghal, Galway, and Limerick.

Though no assay offices were authorised outside Dublin (except for one at Waterford to deal with watch cases in 1784 and never apparently put to use) there were guilds in provincial cities. At Cork, goldsmiths were incorporated with other trades in 1656, but most of their records were destroyed in 1891 in a fire at the Courthouse. The names and marks of many Cork goldsmiths are, however, known from the mid-17th century until the beginning of Queen Victoria's reign. A castle, sometimes accompanied by a ship, was used until the early 18th century, when most silversmiths appear to have used their own name punch and the word Sterling or Starling. In Limerick, too, a castle mark was used, from about 1660 to 1710, but after that Sterling in one form or another was usual. Youghal was also identified by a ship mark, a local yawl, and maritime connections were also indicated by the anchor of Galway, used from about 1660 to 1730.

In Ireland, as in England and Scotland, and in the British territories overseas, research goes on, and much still remains to be done in identifying both town marks and maker's marks, and in adding to the small but increasing knowledge of silversmithing in the provinces.

The Use and Abuse of Hall-marks

Obviously hall-marks are a godsend to the silver collector, an invaluable guide to the quality of the metal, the date, the provenance and the maker. But too much reliance on hall-marks, taken at their face value without reference to the piece on which they appear, can be dangerous, and may even lay the collector open to the wiles of the forger.

In reading hall-marks, care should be taken in looking at the shape of the shields, or outlines of the punch; the style of the town mark and the standard mark; the style of the date letter and the actual appearance and crispness of the marks, as well as their position on the piece. Hall-marks are struck with very carefully made dies that leave a sharp impression when they are first punched, and even long years of wear will not usually leave a "soft" appearance which is one of the signs of the faker, who is not usually prepared to spend the time and money making high-grade dies. This is not to say that all "rubbed" marks are suspect, though one should immediately be suspicious of fairly good Britannia marks with very rubbed maker's marks and date letter. Incidentally, very few makers' marks are as crisply struck as the official hall-marks. The placing of the marks is also an important guide: a London-made tankard and cover of 17th century date would have the marks to the right of the handle, near the rim, and another set across the top of the flat cap cover. A mid-18th century one would have the marks on the base. Spoons and forks until 1780 had "bottom marks" near the bowl end, after that they were placed near the end of the stem.

Not all good antique silver bears full hall-marks. Some is completely unmarked, some bears the maker's mark only, struck once or several times. In itself, the maker's mark is not a guarantee of quality, though the assay office at the period could easily have traced the maker from their registers, and many pieces made to special order were not sent for assay due to an interpretation of the law which suggested that only goods "set for sale" were liable for assay. In some instances, the assay offices themselves made errors, omitting, say, the date letter and striking the lion passant twice. But on a fully marked piece, one would expect full marks on the main section, and at least the maker's mark and usually also the lion passant on minor parts, such as the lid of a tankard or coffee pot.

makers mark   standard mark   assay mark   date letter

The status of the hall-mark led to many imitations of it, first among the pewterers and later, in the mid-18th century, by the makers of plated goods. Many marks on Old Sheffield Plate, on close-plated wares and, from about 1860, on electro-plated wares, somewhat resemble silver marks. The imitation marks on Sheffield fused plate in the later 18th century led to restrictions on the type of mark that the platers could register, and most Sheffield Plate marks after 1784 include the maker's full name. Electro-plated wares sometimes also carry hall-mark-like stamps, but often the letters EP, EPNS or EPBM for nickel plated, and Britannia metal wares can be detected, and careful examination of the piece will usually reveal the base metal core.

The reason for hall-marking is to protect the public (in other words, the purchasers) against fraud. However, the long history of hall-marking has resulted in a whole variety of styles of marking, together with some confusing legislation.

The 1973 Hall-marking Act resulted in simplification of the marks, making them easier to recognise and comprehend. In addition, certain other important changes were introduced. One of these was that from 1st January, 1975, platinum had to carry marks. Another change meant that the weight threshold for marking an article is now as follows: silver 7·8g; gold 1g; platinum 0·5g.

British hall-marks consist of a registered sponsor's (maker's) mark, together with the Standard Mark, the Assay Mark and Date Letter (see tables below). Note that Edinburgh uses the Lion Rampant for sterling silver.

THE MARKS ON GOLD

Most of the Statutes regulating hall-marking applied equally to gold, and the marks used were the same as those on silver until 1798, though the standard was changed from time to time. In 1477 it was reduced from 19·2 ct. to 18 ct., but in 1575 it was raised to 22 ct., at which it remained until 1798, being marked with the maker's mark, the lion passant, the assay office mark and the date letter with the sovereign's head duty mark also from 1784. A major change in gold marking in England occurred in 1798, when both 18 ct. and 22 ct. gold were permitted, and were indicated by the relevant figures and by a crown, which replaced the lion passant standard mark. In 1854 three lower standards were introduced, and these were indicated by the carat number plus the value in decimals: 9 with ·375; 12 with ·5 and 15 with ·625. In 1931, 12 ct. and 15 ct. were replaced by 14 ct. (·585) and the crown mark since 1854 has been reserved for the higher 18 ct. and 22 ct. standards. In Sheffield, which obtained a licence to assay goldwares in 1903, the gold mark is a rose (to avoid confusion with the town mark used on silver). In Edinburgh, the Thistle replaces the crown on 18 ct. and 22 ct. gold, while in Glasgow, until its closure in 1964, the Lion Rampant appeared on all permitted standards.

Ireland from 1784 had three standards for gold – 22 ct.

marked with the figures and with the crowned harp and Hibernia; 20 ct. indicated by figures and with a plume of feathers also: and 18 ct. with the figures and a unicorn's head. The crowned harp was omitted from the lower standard goldwares, and on jewellery.

makers mark   *assay mark*   *gold marks*   *date letter*

GOLD MARKS

GOLD STANDARD MARKS				ASSAY OFFICES	
British		**Imported**		**British**	**Imported**
🟢 916		916		🐱	🔗
22 carat		*22 carat*		*London*	
👑 750		750		⚓	△
18 carat		*18 carat*		*Birmingham*	
👑 585		585		🌹	Ω
14 carat		*14 carat*		*Sheffield*	
👑 375		375		🏰	X
9 carat		*9 carat*		*Edinburgh*	

GOLD MARKS

IRISH STANDARD MARKS

22 carat

20 carat

IRISH IMPORTED

22 carat

IRISH STANDARD MARKS

IRISH IMPORTED

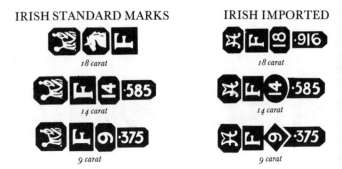

18 carat

18 carat

14 carat

14 carat

9 carat

9 carat

The Marks on Platinum

Since the introduction of legislation following the 1973 Hall-marking Act all articles containing platinum at 950 parts per 1000 or more must be hall-marked. Alloys below this standard may not be described as platinum.

The first year for marking platinum was 1975, starting with the letter 'A'.

makers mark

platinum mark

assay mark

date letter

PLATINUM MARKS

STANDARD MARKS

British   Imported

ASSAY OFFICES

British   Imported

London

Birmingham

Sheffield

ASSAY OFFICE DATE LETTERS

1544	G			
1545	H			Henry VIII
1546	(letter I)			1547 Edward VI
1547	K			1553 Mary
1548	L			
1549	M			G
1550	N			
1551	O			
1552	P			
1553	Q			
1554	R			
1555	S			
1556	T			
1557	V			

Eliz. I	1558	1564		1572	
	1559	1565		1573	
	1560	1566		1574	
	1561	1567		1575	
	1562	1568		1576	
	1563	1569		1577	
		1570			
		1571			

Eliz. I	1578	1585		1592	
	1579	1586		1593	
	1580	1587		1594	
	1581	1588		1595	
	1582	1589		1596	
	1583	1590		1597	
	1584	1591			

Eliz. I **1603** **James I**	1598	1605		1613	
	1599	1606		1614	
	1600	1607		1615	
	1601	1608		1616	
	1602	1609		1617	
	1603	1610			
	1604	1611			
		1612			

LONDON

1618	a	1625	h	James I
1619	b	1626	i	1625
1620	c	1627	k	Charles I
1621	d	1628	l	
1622	e	1629	m	
1623	f	1630	n	
1624	g	1631	o	
		1632	p	a

1633	q
1634	r
1635	s
1636	t
1637	v

1638	a	1645	B	Charles I
1639	B	1646	J	1649
1640	C	1647	B	Charles II
1641	D	1648	E	
1642	E	1649	W	
1643	ff	1650	R	
1644	O	1651	X	a

1652	P
1653	Q
1654	B
1655	O
1656	J
1657	B

1658	A	1665	H	Charles II
1659	B	1666	J	
1660	C	1667	R	
1661	D	1668	L	
1662	E	1669	M	
1663	F	1670	N	
1664	G	1671	O	a

1672	P
1673	D
1674	R
1675	S
1676	T
1677	U

Charles II 1678 1679 1680 1681 1682	(crown) (lion) 1678 (u) 1679 (b) (crown) (lion) 1680 (c) 1681 (d) 1682 (e)		1683 (f) 1684 (g) 1685 (h) 1686 (i) 1687 (k) 1688 (l) 1689 (m) 1690 (n)		1691 (o) 1692 (p) 1693 (q) 1694 (r) 1695 (s) 1696 (t) 1697 (t)	

1685 James II
1689 Wm. & My.
1694 William III

William III 1697 1698 1699 1700 1701	(Britannia) (lion) 1697 (a) (b) 1698 (C) (Britannia) (lion) 1699 (G) 1700 (E) 1701 (F)	1702 (crowned) 1703 (B) 1704 (D) 1705 (S) 1706 (E) 1707 (G) 1708 (H) 1709 (I)	1710 (K) 1711 (L) 1712 (M) 1713 (N) 1714 (O) 1715 (P)	

1702 Anne
1714 George I

George I 1716 1717 1718 1719 1720	(Britannia) (lion) 1716 (A) 1717 (B) 1718 (C) 1719 (D) (crown) (lion) 1720 (E)	(crown) (lion) 1721 (F) 1722 (G) 1723 (H) (crown) (lion) 1724 (I) 1725 (K)	Though not compulsory after 1720, the Britannia Standard was sometimes used as an alternative standard. The identifying marks are to be found between 1720 and the present time. A piece of Britannia Silver assayed in 1721 would therefore carry the marks: (Britannia) (lion) (F)

24

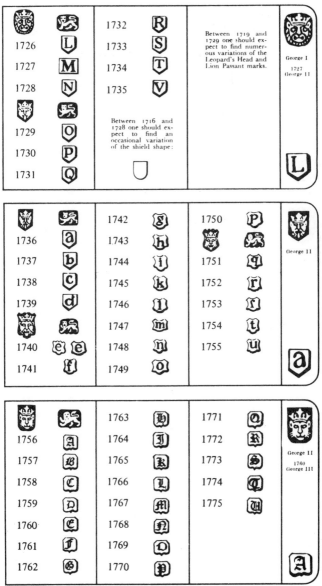

Column 1 (1726–1735):

Year	Mark
1726	L
1727	M
1728	N
1729	O
1730	P
1731	Q

Column 2 (1732–1735):

Year	Mark
1732	R
1733	S
1734	T
1735	V

Between 1716 and 1728 one should expect to find an occasional variation of the shield shape:

Between 1719 and 1729 one should expect to find numerous variations of the Leopard's Head and Lion Passant marks.

George I
1727
George II

Second block:

Year	Mark
1736	a
1737	b
1738	c
1739	d
1740	e e
1741	f
1742	g
1743	h
1744	i
1745	k
1746	l
1747	m
1748	n
1749	o
1750	p
1751	q
1752	r
1753	s
1754	t
1755	u

George II

Third block:

Year	Mark
1756	A
1757	B
1758	C
1759	D
1760	E
1761	F
1762	G
1763	H
1764	J
1765	K
1766	L
1767	M
1768	N
1769	O
1770	P
1771	Q
1772	R
1773	S
1774	T
1775	U

George II
1760
George III

LONDON

George III	1776 **a**	1783 **h**	1791 **q**
	1777 **b**	1784 **i**	1792 **r**
	1778 **c**	1785 **k**	1793 **s**
	1779 **d**	1786 **l**	1794 **t**
	1780 **e**	1787 **m**	1795 **u**
	1781 **f**	1788 **n**	
a	1782 **g**	1789 **o**	An alternative shield may be found.
		1790 **p**	

George III	1796 **A**	1803 **H**	1811 **Q**
	1797 **B**	1804 **I**	1812 **R**
	1798 **C**	1805 **K**	1813 **S**
	1799 **D**	1806 **L**	1814 **T**
	1800 **E**	1807 **M**	1815 **U**
	1801 **F**	1808 **N**	
A	1802 **G**	1809 **O**	An alternative shield may be found.
		1810 **P**	

George III 1820 George IV 1830 William IV	1816 **a**	1821 **f**	1828 **n**
	1817 **b**	1822 **g**	1829 **o**
	1818 **c**	1823 **h**	1830 **p**
	1819 **d**	1824 **i**	1831 **q**
	1820 **e**	1825 **k**	1832 **r**
		1826 **l**	1833 **s**
a		1827 **m**	1834 **t**
			1835 **u**

			1843	🄷	1851	🄠	
1836	🄰		1844	🄹	1852	🄡	William IV
1837	🄱		1845	🄺	1853	🄢	1837 Victoria
1838	🄲		1846	🄻	1854	🄣	
1839	🄳		1847	🄼	1855	🄤	
1840	🄴		1848	🄽			
1841	🄵		1849	🄾	An alternative shield may be found.		
1842	🄶		1850	🄿	⬭		🄰

			1863	🄗	1871	🄠	
1856	🄐		1864	🄘	1872	🄡	Victoria
1857	🄑		1865	🄚	1873	🄢	
1858	🄒		1866	🄛	1874	🄣	
1859	🄓		1867	🄜	1875	🄤	
1860	🄔		1868	🄝			
1861	🄕		1869	🄞	An alternative shield may be found.		
1862	🄖		1870	🄟	⬭		🄐

			1883	🄷			1891	🄠	
1876	🄰		1884	🄸			1892	🄡	Victoria
1877	🄱		1885	🄺			1893	🄢	
1878	🄲		1886	🄻			1894	🄣	
1879	🄳		1887	🄼			1895	🄤	
1880	🄴		1888	🄽					
1881	🄵		1889	🄾					
1882	🄶		1890	🄿					🄰

LONDON

Victoria			1903	h	1911	q
1901 Ewd. VII	1896	a	1904	i	1912	r
1910 George V	1897	b	1905	k	1913	s
	1898	c	1906	l	1914	t
	1899	d	1907	m	1915	u
	1900	e	1908	n		
	1901	f	1909	o		
a	1902	g	1910	p		

George V			1923	h	1931	q
	1916	a	1924	i	1932	r
	1917	b	1925	k	1933	s
	1918	c	1926	l		
	1919	d	1927	m	1934	t
	1920	e	1928	n	1935	u
	1921	f	1929	o	The Britannia Standard Marks for 1927	
a	1922	g	1930	p		

1936 Ewd. VIII			1943	H	1951	Q
1936 George VI	1936	A	1944	I		
1952 Eliz. II	1937	B	1945	K	1952	R
	1938	C	1946	L	1953	S
	1939	D	1947	M		
	1940	E	1948	N	1954	T
	1941	F	1949	O	1955	U
A	1942	G	1950	P		

28

LONDON

🦁 😺	1963	*h*	1971	*q*	😺
1956	*a*	1964	*i*	1972	*r*	Eliz. II
1957	*b*	1965	*k*	This sequence was discontinued after the 1973 Hall-Marking Act	
1958	*c*	1966	*l*		
1959	*d*	1967	*m*	1973	*s*	
1960	*e*	1968	*n*	1974	*t*	
1961	*f*	1969	*o*		
1962	*g*	1970	*p*		*a*

🦁 😺	1982	*H*	1990	*Q*	😺
1975	*A*	1983	*J*		
1976	*B*	1984	*K*		
1977	*C* 👤	1985	*L*		
1978	*D*	1986	*M*		
1979	*E*	1987	*N*		
1980	*F*	1988	*O*		
1981	*G*	1989	*P*		*A*

BIRMINGHAM

George III	1773	A	1781	I	1790	S
	1774	B	1782	K	1791	T
	1775	C	1783	L	1792	U
	1776	D	1784	M	1793	V
	1777	E	1785	N	1794	W
	1778	F	1786	O	1795	X
	1779	G	1787	P	1796	Y
A	1780	H	1788	Q	1797	Z
			1789	R		

July '97 to March '80. The King's Head is duplicated.

George III	1798	a	1806	i	1815	r
1820 George IV	1799	b	1807	j	1816	s
	1800	c	1808	k	1817	t
	1801	d	1809	l	1818	u
	1802	e	1810	m	1819	v
	1803	f	1811	n	1820	w
	1804	g	1812	o	1821	x
a	1805	h	1813	p	1822	y
			1814	q	1823	z

George IV	1824	A	1832	J	1841	S
1830 William IV	1825	B	1833	K	1842	T
1837 Victoria	1826	C	1834	L	1843	U
	1827	D	1835	M	1844	V
	1828	E	1836	N	1845	W
	1829	F	1837	O	1846	X
	1830	G	1838	P	1847	Y
A	1831	H	1839	Q	1848	Z
			1840	R		

30

BIRMINGHAM

Lion / Anchor / Head		Date	Letter	Lion / Anchor / Head		Date	Letter	Anchor
		1849	A			1858	J	Victoria
		1850	B			1859	K	
		1851	C			1860	L	
		1852	D			1861	M	
		1853	E			1862	N	
		1854	F			1863	O	
		1855	G			1864	P	
		1856	H			1865	Q	
		1857	I			1866	R	

	Date	Letter
Lion / Anchor / Head	1867	S
	1868	T
	1869	U
	1870	V
	1871	W
	1872	X
	1873	Y
	1874	Z

Victoria — Anchor — A

1875	a	1883	i	1891	r
1876	b	1884	k	1892	s
1877	c	1885	l	1893	t
1878	d	1886	m	1894	u
1879	e	1887	n	1895	v
1880	f	1888	o	1896	w
1881	g	1889	p	1897	x
1882	h	1890	q	1898	y
				1899	z

Victoria — Anchor — a

BIRMINGHAM

Victoria / 1901 Ewd. VII / 1910 George V					
1900	a	1908	i	1917	s
1901	b	1909	k	1918	t
1902	c	1910	l	1919	u
1903	d	1911	m	1920	v
1904	e	1912	n	1921	w
1905	f	1913	o	1922	x
1906	g	1914	p	1923	y
1907	h	1915	q	1924	z
		1916	r		

George V / 1936 Ewd. VIII					
1925	A	1933	J	1940	Q
1926	B	1934	K	1941	R
1927	C	1935	L	1942	S
1928	D	1936	M	1943	T
1929	E	1937	N	1944	U
1930	F	1938	O	1945	V
1931	G	1939	P	1946	W
1932	H			1947	X
				1948	Y
				1949	Z

BIRMINGHAM

1950	A
1951	B

1952	C
1953	D

1954	E
1955	F
1956	G
1957	H
1958	I
1959	K
1960	L
1961	M
1962	N
1963	O
1964	P
1965	Q

George VI

1952
Eliz. II

1966	R
1967	S
1968	T
1969	U
1970	V
1971	W
1972	X

1973	Y

1974	Z

Eliz. II

1975	A
1976	B
1977	C

1978	D
1979	E
1980	F
1981	G
1982	H
1983	I
1984	K
1985	L
1986	M
1987	N
1988	O
1989	P
1990	Q

STER LING	1680	1690	1690 to 1700	
Charles II 1685 James II 1689 Wm. & My. 1694 William III				

William III 1702 Anne 1714 George I	1701 **A**	1709 **I**	1718 **S**
	1702 **B**	1710 **K**	1719 **T**
	1703 **C**	1711 **L**	1720 **U**
	1704 **D**	1712 **M**	1721 **V**
	1705 **E**	1713 **N**	1722 **W**
	1706 **F**	1714 **O**	1723 **X**
	1707 **G**	1715 **P**	1724 **Y**
	1708 **H**	1716 **Q**	1725 **Z**
		1717 **R**	

George I 1727 George II	1726 **A**	1734 **J**	1743 **S**
	1727 **B**	1735 **K**	1744 **T**
	1728 **C**	1736 **L**	1745 **U**
	1729 **D**	1737 **M**	1746 **V**
	1730 **E**	1738 **N**	1747 **W**
	1731 **F**	1739 **O**	1748 **X**
	1732 **G**	1740 **P**	1749 **Y**
	1733 **H**	1741 **Q**	1750 **Z**
		1742 **R**	

CHESTER

🦁 👑 🛡	1759	i	1768	S		🛡
1751 a	1760	k	1769	T		
1752 b	1761	l	1770	T		👑
1753 c	1762	m	1771	U		
1754 d	1763	n	1772	V		George II
1755 e	1764	o	1773	W		1760 George III
1756 f	1765	p	1774	X		
1757 G	1766	Q	1775	Y		
1758 h	1767	R				a

🦁 👑 🛡	1782	g	1789	O		🛡
1776 a	1783	h	1790	P		
1777 b	🦁 👑 🛡 ♟	1791	q		👑
1778 c	1784	i	1792	r		George III
🦁 👑 🛡	1785	k	1793	S		
1779 d	1786	l ♟	1794	t		
1780 e	1787	m	1795	u		
1781 f	1788	n	1796	v		a

🦁 👑 🛡 ♟	1803	G	1811	P		🛡
1797 A	1804	H	1812	Q		
1798 B	1805	I	1813	R		👑
1799 C	1806	K	1814	S		George III
🦁 👑 🛡 ♟	1807	L	1815	T		
1800 D	1808	M	1816	U		
1801 E	1809	N	1817	V		
1802 F	1810	O				A

George III / 1820 George IV / 1830 William IV / 1837 Victoria	1818 Ā	1824 F	1833 P
	1819 B	1825 G	1834 Q
	1820 C	1826 H	1835 R
	1821 D	1827 I	1836 S
	1822 D	1828 K	1837 T
	1823 E	1829 L	1838 U
		1830 M	
		1831 N	
		1832 O	

Victoria	1839 A	1847 J	1856 S
	1840 B	1848 K	1857 T
	1841 C	1849 L	1858 U
	1842 D	1850 M	1859 V
	1843 E	1851 N	1860 W
	1844 F	1852 O	1861 X
	1845 G	1853 P	1862 Y
	1846 H	1854 Q	1863 Z
		1855 R	

Victoria	1864 a	1871 h	1879 q
	1865 b	1872 i	1880 r
	1866 c	1873 k	1881 s
	1867 d	1874 l	1882 t
	1868 e	1875 m	1883 u
	1869 f	1876 n	
	1870 g	1877 o	
		1878 p	

CHESTER

1884	A	1890	G	1897 O
1885	B	1891	H	1898 P
1886	C	1892	I	1899 Q
1887	D	1893	K	1900 R
1888	E	1894	L	
1889	F	1895	M	
		1896	N	

Victoria

An alternative sterling mark used since 1839.

An alternative date letter shield used since 1900.

1901	A	1908	K	1917 R
1902	B	1909	I	1918 S
1903	G	1910	K	1919 T
1904	D	1911	L	1920 U
1905	E	1912	M	1921 V
1906	F	1913	N	1922 W
1907	G	1914	O	1923 X
		1915	P	1924 Y
		1916	Q	1925 Z

Ewd. VII

1910 George V

1926	a	1933	h	1940 P
1927	b	1934	J	1941 Q
1928	c	1935	R	1942 R
1929	d	1936	k	1943 S
1930	e	1937	w	1944 T
1931	ff	1938	n	1945 U
1932	g	1939	o	1946 V
				1947 W

George V

1936 Ewd. VIII

1936 George VI

| | George VI | 1948 | 1949 | 1950 | 1951 | 1952 | 1953 | 1954 | 1955 | 1956 | 1957 | 1958 | 1959 | 1960 | 1961 | 1962 |

George VI **1952** Eliz. II	1948 **ℵ**	1954 **D**	1961 **L** 1962 **M**
	1949 **Y**	1955 **E**	
	1950 **Z**	1956 **F**	In August of 1962 the Chester Assay Office closed.
	1951 **A**	1957 **G**	
	1952	1958 **H**	
ℵ	1953 **B** 1953 **C**	1959 **J** 1960 **K**	

38

DUBLIN

		1645	H	1652	P	
				1653	Q	
1638	A	1646	I/J	1654	R	
1639	B	1647	K			Charles I
1640	C	1648	L	1655	S	1649 Charles II
1641	D	1649	M	1656	T	
1642	E	1650	N	1657	U	
1643	F	1651	O			
1644	G					A

1658	a	1665	h	1672	p	
1659	b	1666	i	1673	q	
1660	c	1667	k	1674	r	Charles II
1661	d	1668	l	1675	s	
1662	e	1669	m	1676	t	
1663	f	1670	n	1677	u	
1664	g	1671	o			a

1678	A	1688-93	h	1704	R	
1679	B	1694-5	K	1706-7	S	Charles II
1680	C	1696-8	L	1708-9	T	1685 James II
1681	D	1699	M	1710-11	U	1689 Wm. & My.
1682	E	1700	N	1712-13	W	1694 William III
1683-4	F	1701	O	1714	X	1702 Anne
1685-7	G	1702	P	1715	Y	1714 George I
		1703	Q	1716	Z	A

DUBLIN

George I / 1727 George II			1726	Ⓖ	1736	Ⓠ
	1717	Ⓐ	1727	Ⓗ	1737	Ⓡ
	1718	Ⓑ	1728	Ⓙ	1738	Ⓢ
	1719	Ⓒ	1729	Ⓚ	1739	Ⓣ
			1730	Ⓛ	1740	Ⓤ Ⓤ
	1720	Ⓐ	1731	Ⓔ	1741-2	Ⓦ Ⓦ
	1721	Ⓑ	1731	Ⓥ	1743-4	Ⓧ
	1722	Ⓒ	1732	Ⓝ	1745	Ⓨ
	1723	Ⓓ	1733	Ⓝ	1746	Ⓩ
	1724	Ⓔ	1734	Ⓞ	An alternative Crowned Harp found between 1739 and 1748.	
	1725	Ⓕ	1735	Ⓟ		

George II / 1760 George III			1757	Ⓘ	1766	Ⓢ
	1747	Ⓐ	1758	Ⓚ		
			1759	Ⓛ	1767	Ⓣ
	1748	Ⓑ			1768	Ⓤ
	1749	Ⓒ	1760	Ⓜ	1769	Ⓦ
	1750	Ⓓ	1761	Ⓝ	1770	Ⓧ
	1751	Ⓔ Ⓔ	1762	Ⓞ	1771	Ⓨ
	1752	Ⓕ	1763	Ⓟ	1772	Ⓩ
	1753	Ⓖ	1764	Ⓠ	An alternative Hibernia found between 1752 and 1754.	
	1754	Ⓗ	1765	Ⓡ		

DUBLIN

🏛️ 👑	1781	Ĩ	1790	Ŝ	👑
1773	A	1782	K̃	1791	T̃	
1774	B	1783	L̃	1792	Ũ	🧍
1775	C	1784	M̃	🧍 👑		George III
🏛️ 👑	1785	Ñ	1793	W̃	
1776	D	1786	Õ	1794	X̃	
1777	E	🏛️ 👑	1795	Ỹ	
1778	F	1787	P̃	1796	Z̃	
1779	G	1788	Q̃		
1780	H	1789	R̃		A

🧍 👑	1806	K	1815	T̃	👑
1797	A	1807	L 👤	1816	Ũ	
1798	B	1808	M	1817	W̃	🧍
1799	C	1809	N 👤	1818	X̃	George III
1800	D	🧍 👑 👤	1819	Ỹ	1820 George IV
1801	E	1810	Õ	1820	Z̃	
1802	F	1811	P̃		
1803	G	1812	Q̃		
1804	H	1813	R̃		
1805	I	1814	S̃		A

41

	Date	Letter			
	1821	Ⓐ	🏵	🏵	👤
	1822	Ⓑ			👤
	1823	Ⓒ			
	1824	Ⓓ			
1820 George IV	1825	Ⓔ ⓔ			
1830 William IV	1826	Ⓕ			
1837 Victoria	1827	Ⓖ	🏵	🏵	👤
	1828	Ⓗ	🏵	🏵	👤
	1829	Ⓘ	🏵	🏵	👤
	1830	Ⓚ	🏵	🏵	👤
	1831	Ⓛ	🏵	🏵	👤
	1832	Ⓜ			
	1833	Ⓝ	🏵	🏵	
	1834	Ⓞ	🏵	🏵	👤
	1835	Ⓟ			
	1836	Ⓠ			
	1837	Ⓡ	🏵	🏵	👤
	1838	Ⓢ			👤
	1839	Ⓣ	🏵	🏵	
	1840	Ⓤ			
	1841	Ⓥ			
	1842	Ⓦ	🏵	🏵	
	1843	Ⓧ			
	1844	Ⓨ	🏵	🏵	
	1845	Ⓩ	🏵		🏵

Ⓐ

DUBLIN

1846	â	1855	k	1864	t		Victoria
1847	b	1856	l	1865	u		
1848	c	1857	m	1866	v		
1849	d	1858	n	1867	w		
1850	e	1859	o	1868	x		
1851	f f	1860	p	1869	y		
1852	g g	1861	q	1870	z		
1853	h h	1862	r				
1854	j	1863	s				â

1871	A	1880	K	1890	U	Victoria
1872	B	1881	L	1891	V	
1873	C	1882	M	1892	W	
1874	D	1883	N	1893	X	
1875	E	1884	O	1894	Y	
1876	F	1885	P	1895	Z	
1877	G	1886	Q			
1878	H	1887	R			
1879	I	1888	S			
		1889	T			A

	1896 Ⓐ	1902	Ⓖ	1909	Ⓞ

		1902 Ⓖ	1909 Ⓞ
	1896 Ⓐ	1903 Ⓗ	1910 Ⓟ
	1897 Ⓑ	1904 Ⓙ	1911 Ⓠ
Victoria	1898 Ⓒ	1905 Ⓚ	1912 Ⓡ
1901 Ewd. VII	1899 Ⓓ	1906 Ⓛ	1913 Ⓢ
1910 George V	1900 Ⓔ	1907 Ⓜ	1914 Ⓣ
Ⓐ	1901 Ⓕ	1908 Ⓝ	1915 Ⓤ

		1925 Ⓑ	1935 Ⓣ
	1916 Ⓐ	1926 Ⓛ	1936 Ⓤ
	1917 Ⓑ	1927 Ⓜ	1937 Ⓥ
George V	1918 Ⓒ	1928 Ⓝ	1937 Ⓥ
1936 Ewd. VIII	1919 Ⓓ	1929 Ⓞ	1938 Ⓦ
1936 George VI	1920 Ⓔ	1930 Ⓟ	1939 Ⓧ
	1921 Ⓕ	1931 Ⓟ	1940 Ⓨ
	1922 Ⓢ	1932 Ⓠ	1941 Ⓩ
	1923 Ⓗ	1933 Ⓡ	
Ⓐ	1924 Ⓘ	1934 Ⓢ	

DUBLIN

(harp/figure marks)	1951	**J**	1960	**S**	(harp/figure marks)
1942	**A**	1952	**K**	1961	**T**
1943	**B**	1953	**L**	1962	**U**
1944	**C**	1954	**M**	1963	**V**
1945	**D**	(figure/harp marks)	1964	**W**	George VI
1946	**E**	1955	**N**	1965	**X**	1952 Eliz. II
1947	**F**	1956	**O**	(marks)	
1948	**G**	1957	**P**	1966	**Y**
1949	**H**	1958	**Q**	(marks)	
1950	**I**	1959	**R**	1967	**Z**	**A**

(figure/harp marks)	1976	**l**	1987	*B*	(harp/figure marks)
1968	**a**	1977	**l** (head)	1988	*C*
1969	**b**	1978	**m**	1989	*D*
1970	**c**	1979	**n**	1990	*E*	Eliz. II
1971	**d**	1980	**O**		
1972	**e**	1981	**P**		
1973	**F**	1982	**R**		
(figure/harp marks)	1983	**S**		
1974	**S**	1984	**t**		
		1985	**U**		
1975	**h**	1986	*A*		**a**

EDINBURGH

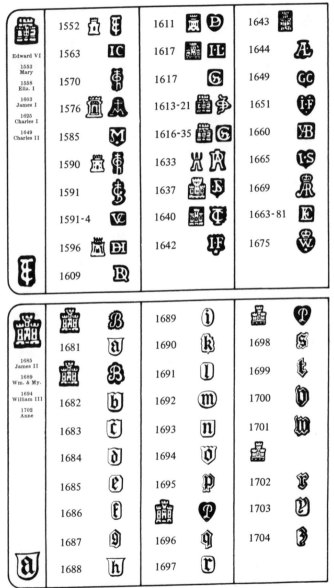

Edward VI	1552		1611	1643	
1553 Mary	1563	IC	1617	IL	1644	A
1558 Eliz. I	1570		1617	G	1649	GC
1603 James I	1576		1613-21		1651	IF
1625 Charles I	1585	M	1616-35	G	1660	VB
1649 Charles II	1590		1633	A	1665	IS
	1591		1637	S	1669	AR
	1591-4	VC	1640	T	1663-81	E
	1596		1642	IF	1675	W
	1609	B				

1685 James II		B	1689	i		P
1689 Wm. & My.	1681	a	1690	k	1698	S
1694 William III		B	1691	l	1699	t
1702 Anne	1682	b	1692	m	1700	v
	1683	c	1693	n	1701	w
	1684	d	1694	o		
	1685	e	1695	p	1702	r
	1686	f		P	1703	y
	1687	g	1696	q	1704	z
	1688	h	1697	r		

46

EDINBURGH

🏰	🅟	1713	I	1721	R	🏰
1705	A	🏰	EP	1722	S	Anne
1706	B	1714	K	1723	T	1714 George I
🏰	EP	1715	L	1724	U	1727 George II
1707	C	1716	M	1725	V	
1708	D	1717	N	1726	W	
1709	E	🏰	EP	1727	X	
1710	F	1718	O	1728	Y	
1711	G	1719	P	1729	Z	
🏰	EP	🏰	EP			
1712	H	1720	q			A

🏰	AU	1739	K	1746	R	🏰
1730	A	🏰	GED	🏰	HG	George II
1731	B	1740	L	1747	S	
1732	C	1741	M	1748	J	
1733	D	🏰	EL	1749	U	
1734	E	1742	N	1750	U	
1735	F	1743	O	1751	W	
1736	G	🏰	HG	1752	X	
1737	H	1744	P	1753	Y	
1738	J	1745	Q	1754	Z	A

EDINBURGH

George II **1760 George III**	H·G	HG			1771	R	
	1755	A	1763	J J	1772	S	
	1756	B	1764	k	1773	T	
	1757	C	1765	L	1774	U	
	1758	D	1766	M	1775	V	
	1759		1767	N	1776	X	
	1760	F	1768	O	1777	Y	
	1761	G	1769	P	1778	Z	
A	1762	H	1770	Q	1779	U	

Alternative town marks sometimes found around 1771.

George III			1789	I J	1798	S	
	1780	A	1790	K	1799	T	
	1781	B	1791	L	1800	U	
	1782	C	1792	M	1801	V	
	1783	D	1793	N N			
	1784	E	1794	O O	1802	W	
	1785	F	1795	P	1803	X	
	1786	G	1796	Q	1804	Y	
	1787	G	1797	R R	1805	Z	
A	1788	H					

		Date	Letter			
		1814	i			George III
1806	a	1815	J	1824	s	1820 George IV
1807	b	1816	k	1825	t	1830 William IV
1808	c	1817	l			
		1818	m	1826	u	
1809	d	1819	n	1827	v	
1810	e			1828	w	
1811	f	1820	o	1829	x	
1812	g	1821	p	1830	y	
		1822	q	1831	z	
1813	h	1823	r			a

		Date	Letter			
1832	A	1841	K	1851	U	William IV
1833	B	1842	L	1852	V	1837 Victoria
1834	C	1843	M	1853	W	
1835	D	1844	N	1854	X	
1836	E	1845	O	1855	Y	
1837	F	1846	P	1856	Z	
1838	G	1847	Q			
1839	H	1848	R			
1840	J	1849	S			
		1850	T			A

Victoria	1857	Ⓐ	1865	Ⓘ	1874	Ⓢ	
	1858	Ⓑ	1866	Ⓚ	1875	Ⓣ	
	1859	Ⓒ	1867	Ⓛ	1876	Ⓤ	
	1860	Ⓓ	1868	Ⓜ	1877	Ⓥ	
	1861	Ⓔ	1869	Ⓝ	1878	Ⓦ	
	1862	Ⓕ	1870	Ⓞ	1879	Ⓧ	
	1863	Ⓖ	1871	Ⓟ	1880	Ⓨ	
Ⓐ	1864	Ⓗ	1872	Ⓠ	1881	Ⓩ	
			1873	Ⓡ			

Victoria 1901 Ewd. VII	1882	ⓐ	1890	ⓘ	1898	ⓡ	
	1883	ⓑ	1891	ⓚ	1899	ⓢ	
	1884	ⓒ	1892	ⓛ	1900	ⓣ	
	1885	ⓓ	1893	ⓜ	1901	ⓥ	
	1886	ⓔ	1894	ⓝ	1902	ⓦ	
	1887	ⓕ	1895	ⓞ	1903	ⓧ	
	1888	ⓖ	1896	ⓟ	1904	ⓨ	
ⓐ	1889	ⓗ	1897	ⓠ	1905	③	

EDINBURGH

🏰	🌿	1914	I	🏰	🌿	🏰	
1906	A	1915	K	1923	S	Ewd. VII	
1907	B	1916	L	1924	T	1910 George V	
1908	C	1917	M	1925	U		
1909	D	1918	N	1926	V		
1910	E	1919	O	1927	W		
1911	F	1920	P	1928	X		
1912	G	1921	Q	1929	Y		
1913	H	1922	R	1930	Z	A	

🏰	🌿	🏰	🌿	1948	𝒮	🏰	
1931	𝒜	1939	𝒥	1949	𝒯	Ewd. VIII	
1932	ℬ	1940	𝒦	1950	𝒰	1936 George VI	
🏰 🌿 ⬤		1941	ℒ	1951	𝒱	1952 Eliz. II	
1933	𝒞	1942	ℳ	🏰 🌿 ⬤			
1934	𝒟	1943	𝒩	1952	𝒲		
1935	ℰ	1944	𝒪	1953	𝒳		
1936	ℱ	1945	𝒫	🏰 🌿			
1937	𝒢	1946	𝒬	1954	𝒴		
1938	ℋ	1947	ℛ	1955	𝒵	𝒜	

			Eliz. II	
			1965	k
Eliz. II	1956	A	1966	l
	1957	B	1967	m
	1958	C	1968	n
	1959	D	1969	o
	1960	E	1970	p
	1961	F	1971	q
	1962	G	1972	r
	1963	H	1973 31st December } 1974	s
A	1964	I		

			1986	M
	1975	A	1987	N
	1976	B	1988	O
	1977	C	1989	P
	1978	D	1990	Q
	1979	E		
	1980	F		
	1981	G		
	1982	H		
	1983	I		
	1984	K		
A	1985	L		

🅧 **IOMS**	⊗	⊞ x⊠c	🅧 **IOMS**
1570	1585 1630	🐿️	Eliz. I
			1603 James I
I **n**	♛ ⊛	🦁 ⊠	1625 Charles I
1571	1635 1675	1690	1649 Charles II
			1685 James II
⊗ ⊞	⊞	ẋ ✤	1689 Wm. & My.
1575	1680	1698	1694 William III
⊗			
1580			

🏰 🧍 🐿️	1709 Ⓘ	1718 Ⓢ	🏰
1701 Ⓐ	1710 Ⓚ	1719 Ⓣ	🧍
1702 Ⓑ	1711 Ⓛ	1720 Ⓥ	Anne
1703 Ⓒ	1712 Ⓜ	🏰 🛡️ 🦁	1714 George I
1704 Ⓓ	1713 Ⓝ	1721 Ⓦ	
1705 Ⓔ	1714 Ⓞ	1722 Ⓧ	
1706 Ⓕ	1715 Ⓟ	1723 Ⓨ	
1707 Ⓖ	1716 Ⓠ	1724 Ⓩ	
1708 Ⓗ	1717 Ⓡ		Ⓐ

		1733	i	1741	r
		1734	k	1742	s
George I	1725	a	1735	l	1743	t
1727 George II	1726	b	1736	m	1744	u
	1727	c	1737	n	1745	w
	1728	d	1738	o	1746	x
	1729	e	1739	p	1747	y
	1730	f	1740	q	1748	z
	1731	g				
	1732	h				

		1757	I	1765	R
	1749	A	1758	K	1766	S
George II	1750	B	1759	L	1767	T
1760 George III	1751	C	1760	M	1768	U
	1752	D	1761	N	1769	W
	1753	E	1762	O	1770	X
	1754	F	1763	P	1771	Y
	1755	G	1764	Q	1772	Z
	1756	H				

		1781	I	1789	g
	1773	A	1782	I	1790	r
George III	1774	B	1783	K	1791	f
	1775	C	1784	L	1792	t
	1776	D	1785	M	1793	u
	1777	E	1786	N	1794	W
	1778	F	1787	O	1795	X
	1779	G	1788	P	1796	y
	1780	H				

🏰 🦁 👤	1804 H	1811 P	🏰 George III
1797 A	🏰 🦁 👤	1812 Q	
1798 B	1805 I	1813 R	
1799 C 👤	1806 K	1814 S	
1800 D	1807 L	1815 T	
1801 E	1808 M	1816 U	
1802 F	1809 N		
1803 G	1810 O		A

🏰 🦁 👤	1824 h	🏰 🦁 👤	🏰 George III
1817 a	1825 i	1831 p	1820 George IV
1818 b	1826 k	1832 q	1830 William IV
1819 c 👤	1827 l	🏰 🦁 👤	
1820 d	1828 m	1833 r	
1821 e	1829 n	1834 s 👤	
1822 f	1830 o	1835 t	
1823 g		1836 u	a

🏰 🦁 👤	🏰 🦁 👤	1850 O	🏰 Victoria
1837 A 👤	1843 G	1851 P	
1838 B 👤	1844 H	1852 Q	
1839 C	1845 J	1853 R	
1840 D	1846 K	1854 S	
🏰 🦁 👤	1847 L	1855 T	
1841 E	1848 M	1856 U	
1842 F	1849 N		A

Victoria [castle]	[shield] [lion] [head]		
	1857 (A)	1864 (H)	1872 (Q)
	1858 (B)	1865 (I)	1873 (R)
	1859 (C)	1866 (K)	1874 (S)
	1860 (D)	1867 (L)	1875 (T)
	1861 (E)	1868 (M)	1876 (U)
	1862 (F)	1869 (N)	
(A)	1863 (G)	1870 (O)	
		1871 (P)	

Victoria [castle]	[shield] [lion] [head]		
	1877 (A)		
	1878 (B)		
	1879 (C)		
	1880 (D)		
	1881 (E)		
(A)	1882 (F)		

GLASGOW

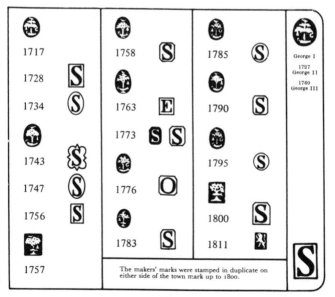

1681 **a**	1694	1700	Charles II
	1696	1701	1685 James II
1683		1704	1689 Wm. & My.
1685	1698	1705	1694 William III
1689		1707 **B**	1702 Anne
1690	1699	1709 **D**	**a**

1717	1758 **S**	1785 **S**	George I
1728 **S**	1763 **E**	1790 **S**	1727 George II
1734 **S**	1773 **S** **S**	1795 **S**	1760 George III
1743 **S**	1776 **O**		
1747 **S**		1800 **S**	
1756 **S**	1783 **S**	1811	
1757	The makers' marks were stamped in duplicate on either side of the town mark up to 1800.		**S**

57

George IV / 1830 William IV / 1837 Victoria	1819	Ⓐ	1827	Ⓘ	1837	Ⓢ
	1820	Ⓑ	1828	Ⓙ	1838	Ⓣ
	1821	Ⓒ	1829	Ⓚ	1839	Ⓤ
	1822	Ⓓ	1830	Ⓛ	1840	Ⓥ
	1823	Ⓔ	1831	Ⓜ	1841	Ⓦ
	1824	Ⓕ	1832	Ⓝ	1842	Ⓧ
	1825	Ⓖ	1833	Ⓞ	1843	Ⓨ
	1826	Ⓗ	1834	Ⓟ	1844	Ⓩ
			1835	Ⓠ		
			1836	Ⓡ		

Victoria	1845	Ⓐ	1853	Ⓘ	1862	Ⓡ
	1846	Ⓑ	1854	Ⓙ	1863	Ⓢ
	1847	Ⓒ	1855	Ⓚ	1864	Ⓣ
	1848	Ⓓ	1856	Ⓛ	1865	Ⓤ
	1849	Ⓔ	1857	Ⓜ	1866	Ⓥ
	1850	Ⓕ	1858	Ⓝ	1867	Ⓦ
	1851	Ⓖ	1859	Ⓞ	1868	Ⓧ
	1852	Ⓗ	1860	Ⓟ	1869	Ⓨ
			1861	Ⓠ	1870	Ⓩ

GLASGOW

🛡️ 🦁 👤	1879	Ⓘ	1888	Ⓡ	🛡️ Victoria
1871	Ⓐ	1880	Ⓙ	1888	Ⓡ
1872	Ⓑ	1881	Ⓚ	1889	Ⓢ
1873	Ⓒ	1882	Ⓛ	1890	Ⓣ
1874	Ⓓ	1883	Ⓜ	1891	Ⓤ
1875	Ⓔ	1884	Ⓝ	1892	Ⓥ
1876	Ⓕ	1885	Ⓞ	1893	Ⓦ
1877	Ⓖ	1886	Ⓟ	1894	Ⓧ
1878	Ⓗ	1887	Ⓠ	1895	Ⓨ
				1896	Ⓩ	Ⓐ

🛡️ 🦁	1906	𝒥	🛡️ 🦁 🛡️	🛡️ Victoria
1897	𝒜	1907	𝒦	1914	ℛ	1901 Ewd. VII
1898	ℬ	1908	𝒵	1915	𝒮	1910 George V
1899	𝒞	1909	ℳ	1916	𝒯
1900	𝒟	1910	𝒩	1917	𝒰
1901	ℰ	1911	𝒬	1918	𝒱
1902	ℱ	1912	𝒫	1919	𝒲
1093	𝒢	1913	𝒜	1920	𝒳
1904	ℋ			1921	𝒴
1905	𝒥			1922	𝒵	𝒜

George V / 1936 Ewd. VIII / 1936 George VI				
1923	a	1932	j	1941	s
1924	b	1933	k	1942	t
1925	c	1934	l	1943	u
1926	d	1935	m	1944	v
1927	e	1936	n	1945	w
1928	f	1937	o	1946	x
1929	g	1938	p	1947	y
1930	h	1939	q	1948	z
1931	i	1940	r		

George VI / 1952 Eliz. II			
1949	A	1956	H
1950	B	1957	J
1951	C	1958	L
1952	D	1959	M
1953	e	1960	N
1954	F	1961	O
1955	G	1962	P
		1963	R

In March 1964 the Glasgow Assay Office closed.

NEWCASTLE

C.1658 to C.1670	C.1685 to C.1694	C.1700	Charles II
C.1672 to C.1684	C.1696		1685 James II
			1689 Wm. & My.
			1694 William III

	1709	1716	
1702 **A**	1710	1717 **P**	1702 Anne
1703 **B**	1711	1718 **D**	
1704 **C**	1712 **D**	1719 **D**	1714 George I
1705 **D**	1713	1720 **E**	
1706 **E**			
1707 **F**	1714 **D**		
1708 **B**	1715		**A**

		1735 **P**	
1721 **a**	1728 **B**	1736 **Q**	
1722 **B**	1729 **F**	1737 **R**	George I
1723 **C**	1730 **K**	1738 **S**	1727 George II
1724 **D**	1731 **L**	1739 **T**	
1725 **E**	1732 **M**		
1726 **F**	1733 **N**	Between 1721 and 1728, the shapes of date shields and lion passant marks often varied. The lion sometimes faces to the left.	**a**
1727 **G**	1734 **D**		

61

George II

Year	Letter
1740	A
1741	B
1742	C
1743	D
1744	E
1745	F
1746	G
1747	H
1748	I
1749	K
1750	L
1751	M
1752	N
1753	O
1754	P
1755	Q
1756	R
1757	S
1758	

George II / 1760 George III

Year	Letter
1759	A
1760 68	B
1769	C
1770	D
1771	E
1772	F
1773	G
1774	H
1775	I
1776	K
1777	L
1778	M
1779	N
1780	O
1781	P
1782	Q
1783	R
1784	S
1785	T
1786	U
1787	W
1788	X
1789	Y
1790	Z

George III

Year	Letter
1791	A
1792	B
1793	C
1794	D
1795	E
1796	F
1797	G
1798	H
1799	I
1800	K
1801	L
1802	M
1803	N
1804	O
1805	P
1806	Q
1807	R
1808	S
1809	T
1810	U
1811	W
1812	X
1813	Y
1814	Z

NEWCASTLE

Assay marks	1815–1822	1823–1830	1831–1838	Sovereign marks
🐟 🛡 🦁 👤	1823 I	1831 R	🛡
1815 A	1824 K	1832 S 👤	🦁
1816 B	1825 L	1833 T	George III
1817 C	1826 M	1834 U	1820 George IV
1818 D	1827 N	1835 W	1830 William IV
1819 E	1828 O	1836 X	1837 Victoria
1820 F	1829 P	1837 Y	
1821 G 👤	1830 Q	1838 Z	A
1822 H			

🐟 🛡 🦁 👤	🐟 🛡 🦁 👤	1855 Q	🛡
1839 A	1846 H	1856 R	🦁
1840 B	1847 I	1857 S	Victoria
1841 C 👤	1848 J	1858 T	
1842 D	1849 K	1859 U	
1843 E	1850 L	1860 W	
1844 F	1851 M	1861 X	
1845 G	1852 N	1862 Y	
	1853 O	1863 Z	A
	1854 P		

🐟 🛡 🦁 👤	1871 h	1879 q	🛡
1864 a	1872 i	1880 r	🦁
1865 b	1873 k	1881 s	Victoria
1866 c	1874 l	1882 t	
1867 d	1875 m	1883 u	
1868 e	1876 n		
1869 f	1877 o		
1870 g	1878 p		a

Eliz. I	1565	**A**	1569	**E**
1603 James I	1566	**B**		
	1567	**C**	1570	**F**
			1571	**G**
			1573	**I**
			1574	**K**
A	1568	**D**	1579	**P**

1590	
1595	
1600	
1610	
1620	

James I	With variations	1630	**G**	1637	**O**
1625 Charles I	1624	**A**	1631	**H**	1638	**P**
	1625	**B**	1632	**I**	1639	**Q**
	1626	**C**	1633	**K**	1640	**R**
	1627	**D**	1634	**L**	1641	**S**
	1628	**E**	1635	**M**	1642	**T**
A	1629	**F**	1636	**N**	1643	**V**

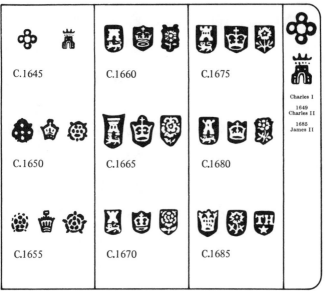

C.1645

C.1650

C.1655

C.1660

C.1665

C.1670

C.1675

C.1680

C.1685

Charles I
1649
Charles II
1685
James II

1688

1689

1691

1696

1697

1701

James II
1689
Wm. & My.
1694
William III

George III	🦁 👑		1782	**G** 👑	1791	**P** 👑	
	1773	**C**	1783	**B** 👑	1792	**U** 👑	
	1774	**F**	1784	**J** 👑	1793	**O** 👑	
	1775	**H**	1785	**P** 👑	1794	**m** 👑	
	1776	**R**		🦁 👑 👤	1795	**q** 👑	
	1777	**h**	1786	**k** 👑	1796	**Z** 👑	
	1778	**S**	1787	**T** 👑	1797	**X** 👤 👑	
	1779	**A**	1788	**W** 👑	1798	**V** 👤 👑	
	1780	**C** 👑	1789	**m** 👑	July '79 to March '80. The King's Head is duplicated.		
	1781	**D** 👑	1790	**L** 👑			

George III 1820 George IV	🦁 👑 👤		1807	**S** 👑	1816	**T** 👑	
	1799	**E** 👑	1808	**P** 👑	1817	**X** 👑	
	1800	**N** 👑	1809	**K** 👑	1818	**I** 👑	
	1801	**H** 👑	1810	**L** 👑	1819	**V** 👑	
	1802	**M** 👑	1811	**C** 👑	1820	**Q** 👑	
	1803	**F** 👑	1812	**D** 👑	1821	**Y** 👑	
	1804	**G** 👑	1813	**R** 👑		🦁 👤 👑	
	1805	**B** 👑	1814	**W** 👑	1822	**Z** 👑	
	1806	**A** 👑	1815	**O** 👑	1823	**U** 👑	

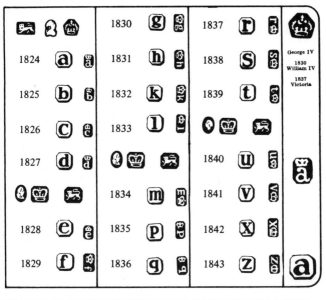

1824 **a**	1830 **g**	1837 **r**
1825 **b**	1831 **h**	1838 **s**
1826 **c**	1832 **k**	1839 **t**
1827 **d**	1833 **l**	1840 **u**
1828 **e**	1834 **m**	1841 **v**
1829 **f**	1835 **p**	1842 **x**
	1836 **q**	1843 **z**

George IV
1830 William IV
1837 Victoria

1844 **A**	1851 **H**	1860 **S**
1845 **B**	1852 **I**	1861 **T**
1846 **C**	1853 **K**	1862 **U**
1847 **D**	1854 **L**	1863 **V**
1848 **E**	1855 **M**	1864 **W**
1849 **F**	1856 **N**	1865 **X**
1850 **G**	1857 **O**	1866 **Y**
	1858 **P**	1867 **Z**
	1859 **R**	

Victoria

Victoria	1868	A	1876	J	1885	S
	1869	B	1877	K	1886	T
	1870	C	1878	L	1887	U
	1871	D	1879	M	1888	V
	1872	E	1880	N	1889	W
	1873	F	1881	O	1890	X
	1874	G	1882	P	1891	Y
A	1875	H	1883	Q	1892	Z
			1884	R		

Victoria 1901 Ewd. VII 1910 George V	1893	a	1901	i	1910	s
	1894	b	1902	k	1911	t
	1895	c	1903	l	1912	u
	1896	d	1904	m	1913	v
	1897	e	1905	n	1914	w
	1898	f	1906	o	1915	x
	1899	g	1907	p	1916	y
a	1900	h	1908	q	1917	z
			1909	r		

SHEFFIELD

1918	a	1926	i	1934	r	George V
1919	b	1927	k	1935	s	
1920	c	1928	l	1936	t	1936 Ewd. VIII / 1936 George VI
1921	d	1929	m	1937	u	
1922	e	1930	n	1938	v	
1923	f	1931	o	1939	w	a
1924	g	1932	p	1940	x	
1925	h	1933	q	1941	y	
				1942	z	

1943	A	1953	L	1964	W	1936 George VI
1944	B	1954	M	1965	X	1952 Eliz. II
1945	C	1955	N	1966	Y	
1946	D	1956	O	1967	Z	
1947	E	1957	P			
1948	F	1958	Q			
1949	G	1959	R			
1950	H	1960	S			
1951	I	1961	T			
1952	K	1962	U			
		1963	V			A

			1974 G	
	1968	A		
	1969	B		
	1970	C		
	1971	D		
	1972	E		
	1973	F		

			1982 H	1990 Q
	1975 A		1983 I	
	1976 B		1984 K	
	1977 C		1985 L	
	1978 D		1986 M	
	1979 E		1987 N	
	1980 F		1988 O	
	1981 G		1989 P	

YORK

During this period several variations of this town mark may be found.				Eliz. I
1562 **D**	1568 **K**		1575 **R**	
1564 **F**	1569 **L**		1576 **S**	
1565 **G**	1570 **M**		1577 **T**	
1566 **H**	1572 **O**		1582 **Z**	
	1573 **P**			
	1574 **Q**			**D**

During this period several variations of this town mark may be found.				Eliz. 1 1603 James 1
1583 **a**	1592 **k**	1596 **o**		
1584 **b**	1593 **l**	1597 **p**		
1587 **e**	1594 **m**	1598 **q**		
1590 **h**	1595 **n**	1599 **r**		
		1601 **t**		
		1604 **x**		**a**

1607 **a**	1615 **J**	1624 **S**	James 1 1625 Charles 1
1608 **B**	1616 **k**	1625 **T**	
1609 **C**	1617 **L**	1626 **U**	
1610 **D**	1618 **M**	1627 **W**	
1611 **E**	1619 **N**	1628 **X**	
1612 **F**	1620 **O**	1629 **Y**	
1613 **G**	1621 **P**	1630 **Z**	
1614 **H**	1622 **Q**		**a**
	1623 **R**		

Charles I / 1649 Charles II	1631	*a*	1638	*h*	1650	*t*
	1632	*b*	1639	*i*	1651	*u*
	1633	*c*	1641	*k*	1652	*v*
	1634	*d*	1642	*l*	1653	*w*
	1635	*e*	1643	*m*	1654	*x*
	1636	*f*	1645	*o*	1655	*y*
	1637	*g*	1649	*s*	1656	*z*

Charles II			1664	*H*	1673	*R*
			1665	*J*	1674	*S*
	1657	*A*	1666	*K*	1675	*T*
	1658	*B*	1667	*L*	1677	*V*
	1659	*C*	1668	*M*	1678	*W*
	1660	*D*	1669	*N*	1679	*X*
	1661	*E*	1670	*O*	1680	*Y*
	1662	*F*	1671	*P*	1681	*Z*
	1663	*G*	1672	*Q*		

Charles II / 1685 James II / 1689 Wm. & My. / 1694 William III			1689	*H*	1696	*P*
	1682	*A*	1690	*J*	1697	*Q*
	1683	*B*	1691	*K*	1698	*R*
	1684	*C*	1692	*L*	1699	*S*
	1685	*D*	1693	*M*		
	1686	*E*	1694	*N*		
	1687	*F*	1695	*O*		
	1688	*G*				

72

1700	1711	1782 G
1701	1713	1783 H
1702	No records for the period 1714 to 1778.	1784 J
1703	1778 C	1785 K
1705	1779 D	1786 L
1706	1780 E	
1708	1781 F	

William III
1702 Anne
1714 George I
1727 George II
1760 George III

1787 A	1795 i	1803 R
1788 B	1796 k	1804 S
1789 C c	1797 L	1805 T
1790 d	1798 M	1806 U
1791 e	1799 N	1807 V
1792 f	1800 O	1808 W
1793 g	1801 P	1809 X
1794 h	1802 Q	1810 Y
	1803 and 1806 sometimes faced right.	1811 Z

George III

1812 a	1820 i	1829 s
1813 b	1821 k	1830 t
1814 c	1822 l	1831 u
1815 d	1823 m	1832 v
1816 e	1824 n	1833 w
1817 f	1825 o	1834 x
1818 g	1826 p	1835 y
1819 h	1827 q	1836 z
	1828 r	

George III
1820 George IV
1830 William IV

	1837 **A**	1844 **H**	1852 **Q**
	1838 **B**	1845 **I**	1853 **R**
Victoria	1839 **C**	1846 **K**	1854 **S**
	1840 **D**	1847 **L**	1855 **T**
	1841 **E**	1848 **M**	1856 **V**
	1842 **F**	1849 **N**	
A	1843 **G**	1850 **O**	
		1851 **P**	

William Abdy London 1784	**WA**	Joseph Angel London 1849	**J·A**
Robt Abercromby London 1739	**R·A**	Peter Archambo London 1720	**AR**
,, ,, 1740	**Ab**		
Stephen Adams London 1813	**SA**	,, ,, 1722	**PA**
		,, ,, 1739	**P·A**
Charles Aldridge & Henry Green London 1775	**C H A G**	Peter Archambo & Peter Meure London 1749	**P A M**
Colline Allen Aberdeen 1748	**CA**	Thomas Bamford London 1719	**Ba**
,, ,, 1748	**CA**		
George Angel London 1850	**GA**	,, ,, 1720	**TB**
,, ,, 1861	**GA**	,, ,, 1739	**TB**
,, ,, 1875	**GA**	Joseph Barbitt London 1703	**BA**
John Angel & George Angel London 1840	**J·A G·A**	,, ,, 1717	**I·B**
Joseph Angel & John Angel London 1831	**J·A I·A**	,, ,, 1739	**JB**
Joseph Angel London 1811	**J·A**	Edward, John & William Barnard London 1846	**E J B W**

John Barnard London 1702		Peter, Ann & William Bateman London 1800	
,, ,, 1720			
,, ,, 1720		,, ,, 1800	
James Le Bas Dublin 1810		Peter & Jonathan Bateman London 1790	
,, ,, 1819		,, ,, 1790	
John Backe London 1700		Peter & William Bateman London 1805	
,, ,, 1720		,, ,, 1805	
Harry Beathume Edinburgh 1704		William Bateman London 1815	
Hester Bateman London 1761		Joseph Bird London 1697	
,, ,, 1774		,, ,, 1697	
,, ,, 1776		,, ,, 1724	
,, ,, 1778		William Bond Dublin 1792	
,, ,, 1789			

George Boothby London 1720		Thos Bradbury and Sons Sheffield 1889	
,, ,, 1720		,, ,, 1892	
,, ,, 1739		Jonathan Bradley London 1697	
James Borthwick Edinburgh 1681		Robert Breading Dublin 1800	
Mathew Boulton Birmingham 1790		,, ,, 1800	
Mathew Boulton & John Fothergill Birmingham 1773		John Bridge London 1823	
Thomas Bolton Dublin 1701		,, ,, 1823	
,, ,, 1701		,, ,, 1823	
,, ,, 1706		Walter Brind London 1748	
Thos Bradbury and Sons Sheffield 1832		,, ,, 1751	
,, ,, 1867		,, ,, 1751	
,, ,, 1878		,, ,, 1781	
,, ,, 1885		Robert Brook Glasgow 1673	

Alexander Brown Dublin 1735		John Chartier London 1698		
George Brydon London 1720		,, ,, 1723		
,, ,, 1720		,, ,, 1723		
William Burwash London 1802		Henry Chawner London 1786		
,, ,, 1803		,, ,, 1787		
,, ,, 1813		William Chawner London 1819		
William Burwash & Richard Sibley London 1805		,, ,, 1820		
		,, ,, 1823		
		,, ,, 1833		
John Cafe London 1742		Francis Clarke Birmingham 1836		
,, ,, 1742		Nicholas Clausen London 1709		
William Cafe London 1757		,, ,, 1720		
Robt Calderwood Dublin 1727		Jonah Clifton London 1703		
,, ,, 1760		,, ,, 1720		
William Charnelhouse London 1703		John Clifton London 1708		

Cocks & Bettridge Birmingham 1806		Edward Cornock London 1723	
Ebenezer Coker London 1739		Augustin Courtauld London 1729	
,, ,, 1745		,, ,, 1739	
,, ,, 1751		Samuel Courtauld London 1746	
Lawrence Coles London 1697		,, ,, 1751	
John Cooke London 1699		Louisa & Samuel Courtauld London 1777	
Mathew Cooper London 1702		Henry Cowper London 1782	
,, ,, 1705		,, ,, 1787	
,, ,, 1720		Paul Crespin London 1720	
Robert Cooper London 1697		,, ,, 1720	
Thomas Corbet London 1699		,, ,, 1739	
,, ,, 1699		,, ,, 1740	
Edward Cornock London 1707		,, ,, 1757	

MAKERS MARKS

Joseph Creswick Sheffield 1777	**IC**	W. & P. Cunningham Edinburgh 1790	**WPC**
Thomas and James Creswick Sheffield 1810	**T&JC**		
Thomas, James and Nathaniel Creswick Sheffield 1862	**TJ&NC**	Louis Cuny London 1703	
,, ,, 1862	**T C J & N**	Thomas Daniel London 1774	**·TD·**
		,, ,, 1775	**TD**
William Cripps London 1743	**W.C**	,, ,, 1783	**TD**
,, ,, 1746	**W·C**	William Davie Edinburgh 1740	**WD**
,, ,, 1751	**W.C**	,, ,, 1740	**WD**
John Crouch London 1808	**J·C**	William Dempster Edinburgh 1742	**W·D**
Francis Crump London 1741	**FC**	William Denny London c. 1697	
,, ,, 1745	**F C**	William Denny & John Barro 1697	
,, ,, 1750	**FC**		
,, ,, 1756	**F·C**	John Denziloe London 1774	
W. & P. Cunningham Edinburgh c.1780	**W& PC**	Isaac Dighton London 1697	
,, 1790	**W·C PC**	John Downes London 1697	

Nicholas Dumee London 1776		Charles Eley London 1825
John East London 1697		William Eley & George Pierpont London 1777
John Eckford London 1698		William Eley London 1778
,, ,, 1720		,, ,, 1785
,, ,, 1725		,, ,, 1790
,, ,, 1725		,, ,, 1795
,, ,, 1739		,, ,, 1795
John Edwards London 1697		,, ,, 1795
John Edwards London 1724		,, ,, 1825
,, ,, 1724		,, ,, 1826
John Edwards London 1739		,, ,, 1826
,, ,, 1753		William, Charles & Henry Eley London 1824
		Elkington, Mason & Co. Sheffield 1859

Maker	Location	Date	Mark
William Elliott	London	1813	WE
John Emes	London	1798	JE
,,	,,	1802	JE
Thomas Evans	London	1774	TE
,,	,,	1779	TE
,,	,,	1782	TE
John Farnell	London	1714	Fa
,,	,,	1720	IF
Thomas Farren	London	1707	FA
,,	,,	1739	TF
John Fawdery	London	1697	FA
,,	,,	1720	I·F
William Fawdery	London	c. 1697	FA
,,	,,	1720	F
,,	,,	1720	FA
Edward Feline	London	1720	Fe
,,	,,	1720	EF
,,	,,	1739	&F
William Fleming	London	c. 1697	FL
Fenton Brothers	Sheffield	1860	JFF &FF
,,	,,	1875	JFF FF
,,	,,	1883	FF SF
,,	,,	1888	SF AJF
,,	,,	1891	SF WS
,,	,,	1896	F.B! LTD

MAKERS MARKS

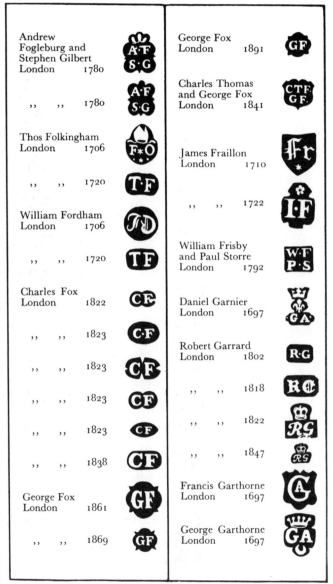

Andrew Fogleburg and Stephen Gilbert London 1780	
,, ,, 1780	
Thos Folkingham London 1706	
,, ,, 1720	
William Fordham London 1706	
,, ,, 1720	
Charles Fox London 1822	
,, ,, 1823	
,, ,, 1823	
,, ,, 1823	
,, ,, 1823	
,, ,, 1838	
George Fox London 1861	
,, ,, 1869	
George Fox London 1891	
Charles Thomas and George Fox London 1841	
James Fraillon London 1710	
,, ,, 1722	
William Frisby and Paul Storre London 1792	
Daniel Garnier London 1697	
Robert Garrard London 1802	
,, ,, 1818	
,, ,, 1822	
,, ,, 1847	
Francis Garthorne London 1697	
George Garthorne London 1697	

Dougal Ged Edinburgh 1734		James Gould London 1739	
Pierre Gillois London 1754		,, ,, 1747	
,, ,, 1782		,, ,, 1748	
James Glen Glasgow 1743		William Gould London 1732	
Elizabeth Godfrey London 1741		,, ,, 1734	
John Goode London 1701		,, ,, 1739	
Andrew Goodwin Dublin 1736		,, ,, 1748	
,, ,, 1739		,, ,, 1753	
Hugh Gordon Edinburgh 1744		Robert Gray & Son Glasgow 1819	
James Gould London 1722		David Green London 1701	
,, ,, 1722		,, ,, 1720	
,, ,, 1732		Henry Greenway London 1775	
		William Gwillim London 1740	

William Gwillim & Peter Castle London 1744	
Hamilton and Inches Edinburgh c. 1880	
John Hamilton Dublin 1717	
,, ,, 1720	
Charles Hancock London 1799	
,, ,, 1814	
Charles Frederick Hancock London 1850	
,, ,, 1850	
,, ,, ·1870	
,, ,, 1870	
John Hardman & Co. Birmingham 1876	
Peter Harrache London 1698	
,, ,, 1698	

Charles Hatfield London 1727	
,, ,, 1727	
,, ,, 1739	
Hawksworth Eyre & Co. Sheffield 1833	
,, ,, 1867	
,, ,, 1869	
,, ,, 1873	
,, ,, 1892	
,, ,, 1894	
Robert Hennell London 1773	
,, ,, 1809	
,, ,, 1820	
,, ,, 1826	
,, ,, 1834 (4th generation)	
Robert & David Hennell London 1795 (3rd generation)	

Robert, David & Samuel Hennell London 1802		John Hodson London 1697	
Robert & Samuel Hennell London 1802		William Holmes and Nicholas Dumee London 1773	
Samuel Hennell London 1811		William Holmes London 1776	
Samuel Hennell and John Terry London 1814		Daniel Holy & Co. Sheffield 1776	
Henry Herbert London 1734		,, ,, 1778	
,, ,, 1735		Samuel Hood London 1697	
,, ,, 1739		,, ,, 1720	
,, ,, 1739		Charles Hougham London 1773	
,, ,, 1747		,, ,, 1785	
,, ,, 1747		,, ,, 1786	
Samuel Herbert London 1747		Francis Howden Edinburgh 1781	
Samuel Herbert & Co. London 1750		Thomas Issod London 1697	

Maker	Location	Date	Mark
John Jacob	London	1734	
,,	,,	1739	
,,	,,	1760	
Joseph Jackson	Dublin	1799	
Charles Kandler	London	1727	
,,	,,	1778	
,,	,,	1778	
Charles Kandler & James Murray	London	1727	
,,	,,	1727	
Charles Frederick Kandler	London	1735	
,,	,,	1735	
Frederick Kandler	London	1739	
Frederick Kandler	London	1758	
Michael Keating	Dublin	1779	
,,	,,	1792	
,,	,,	1854	
William Keats	London	c. 1697	
,,	,,	1697	
,,	,,	1697	
John Keith	Banff	1795	
James Ker	Edinburgh	1723	
David King	Dublin	1706	
,,	,,	1710	
George Lambe	London	1713	
Jonathan Lambe	London	c. 1697	

Paul de Lamerie London 1712		Lea & Clarke Birmingham 1821	L&C
,, ,, 1732		Ledsam, Vale and Wheeler Birmingham 1824	LV&W
,, ,, 1739		George Lewis London 1699	LE
John Lampfert London 1748		Charles Lias London 1837	CL
,, ,, 1749		John, Henry & Charles Lias London 1830	IL HL CL
Louis Laroche London 1725		John & Henry Lias London 1837	I·L H·L
,, ,, 1739		,, ,, 1839	IL HL
Samuel Laundry & Jeffery Griffith London 1731		,, ,, 1843	IL HL
Thomas Law Sheffield 1773	T·LAW	,, ,, 1845	I·L H·L
,, ,, 1773	T·L	Henry John Lias & Henry John Lias London 1850	HL HL
John Lawrence & Co. Birmingham 1826	L&C?	,, ,, 1853	HL HL
Samuel Lea London 1711	LE	,, ,, 1856	HL HL
,, ,, 1721	SL	Isaac Liger London 1704	IL
		,, ,, 1720	IL

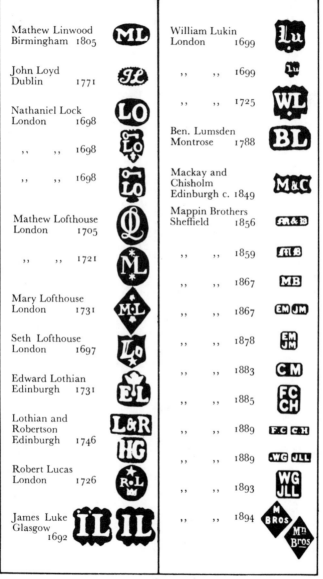

Mathew Linwood Birmingham		1805	
John Loyd Dublin		1771	
Nathaniel Lock London		1698	
,,	,,	1698	
,,	,,	1698	
Mathew Lofthouse London		1705	
,,	,,	1721	
Mary Lofthouse London		1731	
Seth Lofthouse London		1697	
Edward Lothian Edinburgh		1731	
Lothian and Robertson Edinburgh		1746	
Robert Lucas London		1726	
James Luke Glasgow		1692	
William Lukin London		1699	
,,	,,	1699	
,,	,,	1725	
Ben. Lumsden Montrose		1788	
Mackay and Chisholm Edinburgh		c. 1849	
Mappin Brothers Sheffield		1856	
,,	,,	1859	
,,	,,	1867	
,,	,,	1867	
,,	,,	1878	
,,	,,	1883	
,,	,,	1885	
,,	,,	1889	
,,	,,	1889	
,,	,,	1893	
,,	,,	1894	

John Newton Mappin London 1882	JNM	Samuel Margas London 1720	SM
,, ,, ,, 1883	JNM	Thomas Morse London 1720	MO
,, ,, ,, 1884	JNM	,, ,, 1720	TM
,, ,, ,, 1884	J·N·M	Marshall & Son Edinburgh c. 1842	M&S
,, ,, ,, 1885	JNM	Colin McKenzie Edinburgh 1695	MK
,, ,, ,, 1886	JNM	Lewis Mettayer London 1700	ME
John Newton Mappin and George Webb London 1866	JNM GW	,, ,, 1720	LM
,, ,, 1880	J·N·M G.W	Nathaniel Mills Birmingham 1826	NM
Jonathan Madden London 1702	MA	Richard Mills London 1755	R·M
Mathew Madden London 1697	MA	,, ,, 1758	RM
Jacob Margas London 1706	MA	John Moore Dublin 1729	IM
,, . ,, 1720	I·M	,, ,, 1740	IM
Samuel Margas London 1714	MA	,, ,, 1745	M

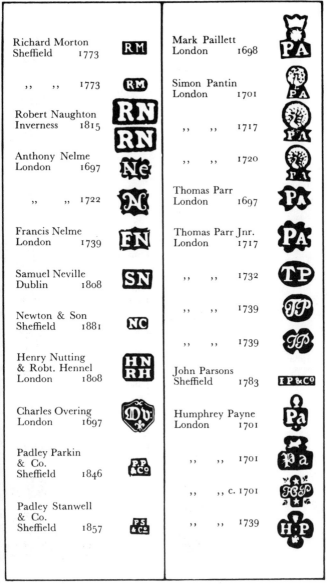

Richard Morton Sheffield 1773	**RM**	
,, ,, 1773	**RM**	
Robert Naughton Inverness 1815	**RN** **RN**	
Anthony Nelme London 1697	**Ne**	
,, ,, 1722	**N**	
Francis Nelme London 1739	**FN**	
Samuel Neville Dublin 1808	**SN**	
Newton & Son Sheffield 1881	**NC**	
Henry Nutting & Robt. Hennel London 1808	**HN** **RH**	
Charles Overing London 1697		
Padley Parkin & Co. Sheffield 1846	**P.P** **& Co**	
Padley Stanwell & Co. Sheffield 1857	**PS** **& Co**	

Mark Paillett London 1698	
Simon Pantin London 1701	
,, ,, 1717	
,, ,, 1720	
Thomas Parr London 1697	
Thomas Parr Jnr. London 1717	
,, ,, 1732	
,, ,, 1739	
,, ,, 1739	
John Parsons Sheffield 1783	**I P & Cº**
Humphrey Payne London 1701	
,, ,, 1701	
,, ,, c. 1701	
,, ,, 1739	

Edmund Pearce London 1704		Peze Pilleau London 1739	
,, ,, 1720		John Pittar Dublin 1751	
William Peaston London 1745		,, ,, 1778	
William and Robert Peaston London 1796		,, ,, 1813	
Samuel Pemberton Birmingham 1784		William Pitts London 1789	
Edward Penman Edinburgh 1706		Pierre Platel London 1699	
James Penman Edinburgh 1705		Philip Platel London 1737	
Phipps & Edward Robinson London 1783		John Pollock London 1734	
		Thomas Powell London 1756	
		,, ,, 1758	
Mathew Pickering London 1703		Joseph Preedy London 1777	
Peze Pilleau London 1720		,, ,, 1800	
,, ,, 1720		John Pringle Perth 1827	
		,, ,, 1827	

Benjamin Pyne London c. 1710		
,, ,, c. 1720		
Phillip Rainaud London 1707		
,, ,, 1720		
John Rand London 1703		
Samuel Roberts Sheffield 1773		
Samuel Roberts Jnr. & George Cadman Sheffield 1786		
,, ,, 1786		
Roberts & Belk Sheffield 1864		
,, ,, 1864		
,, ,, 1892		
,, ,, 1869		
,, ,, 1879		
Patrick Robertson Edinburgh 1751		
John (later Lord) Rollo Edinburgh 1731		
Phillip Rollos London 1697		
,, ,, 1697		
,, ,, 1705		
,, ,, 1720		
Philip Rundell London 1819		
,, ,, 1819		
,, ,, 1822		
Abraham Russell London 1702		
John le Sage London 1722		
,, ,, 1739		
,, ,, 1739		

A. B. Savory London 1826		**A·B·S**
,, ,, 1826		**·ABS·**
,, ,, 1826		**ABS**
,, ,, 1826		**A·B·S**
,, ,, 1826		**ABS**
,, ,, 1826		**ABS**
,, ,, 1836		**A·B·S**
John Schuppe London 1753		**JS**
John Scofield London 1778		**I·S**
,, ,, 1787		**I·S**
Digby Scott and Benjamin Smith London 1802		**D·S & B·S**
,, ,, 1803		**DS BS**
William Scott Banff 1680		**VS**
James Seabrook London 1714		**Se**
,, ,, 1720		**IS**

Daniel Shaw London 1748		**DS**
William Shaw London 1727		**WS**
,, ,, 1728		**SH**
,, ,, 1739		**WS**
,, ,, 1745		**W·S**
,, ,, 1748		**W·S**
William Shaw & William Priest London 1749		**W W·S P**
,, ,, 1750		**W·S P**
W. & G. Sissons Sheffield 1858		**W·S C·S**
Gabriel Sleath London 1706		**SL**
,, ,, 1706		**S·L**
,, ,, 1720		**G·S**
,, ,, 1739		**GS**
Gabriel Sleath & Francis Crump London 1753		**F G·S C**

Benjamin Smith London 1807		Paul Storr London 1807	
Daniel Smith & Robert Sharp London 1780		,, ,, 1808	
,, ,, 1780		,, ,, 1817	
,, ,, 1780		,, ,, 1834	
Edward Smith Birmingham 1833		John Sutton London 1697	
James Smith London 1718		Thomas Sutton London 1711	
,, ,, 1720		John Swift London 1739	
,, ,, 1744		,, ,, 1739	
Stephen Smith London 1865		,, ,, 1757	
,, ,, 1878		James Sympsone Edinburgh 1687	
,, ,, 1880		,, ,, 1687	
Paul Storr London 1799		Richard Syng London 1697	
		,, ,, 1697	

Benjamin Tait Dublin 1791		John Tuite London 1739	
James Tait Edinburgh 1704		William Tuite London 1756	
Ann Tanqueray London 1713		Joseph Turner Birmingham 1838	
David Tanqueray London 1713		George Unite Birmingham c. 1838	
,, ,, 1720		Archibald Ure Edinburgh 1717	
Joseph Taylor Birmingham 1812		Ayme Videau London 1739	
Samuel Taylor London 1744			
Taylor & Perry Birmingham 1834		Edward Vincent London 1739	
Thomas Tearle London 1739		Edward Wakelin London 1747	
Edward Thomason Birmingham 1817		John Wakelin & William Taylor London 1776	
,, ,, 1817		,, ,, 1777	
William Townsend Dublin 1734		Joseph Walker Dublin 1701	
,, ,, 1734			
,, ,, 1753		Samuel Walker Dublin 1738	

MAKERS MARKS

Thomas Walker Dublin 1723		Fuller White London 1750	F·W
Walker Knowles & Co. Sheffield 1836	WK &Co	,, ,, 1758	 FW
Joseph Ward London 1697		John White London 1719	Wh
Samuel Wastell London 170½	W·A	,, ,, 1724	IW
,, ,, 1701	W·A	,, ,, 1730	JW
Mathew West Dublin 1776	MW	George Wicke London 1721	W·I
Gervais Wheeler Birmingham 1835	GW	,, ,, 1721	G W
Thomas Whipham London 1737	T·W	,, ,, 1735	G·W
,, ,, 1739	TW	Starling Wilford London 1717	WI
Thomas Whipham & Charles Wright London 1757	C T·W	,, ,, 1720	SW
Thos. Whipham and Wilm. Williams London 1740	W T·W W	,, ,, 1729	SW
		David Willaume London 1718	WI
Fuller White London 1744	FW	,, ,, 1718	WI
		,, ,, 1728	WI
		,, ,, 1728	DW

David Willaume London 1734		Edward Wood London 1740	
Richard Williams Dublin 1761		Samuel Wood London 1733	
,, ,, 1775		,, ,, 1737	
Wilm. Williamson Dublin 1773		,, ,, 1739	
,, ,, 1747		,, ,, 1754	
Joseph Willmore Birmingham 1806		William Woodard London 1741	
Thomas Willmore Birmingham 1789		John Wren London 1777	
,, ,, 1796		Charles Wright London 1775	
John Winter & Co. Sheffield 1836		,, ,, 1780	
John Wirgman London 1751		James Young London 1775	
Edward Wood London 1722		John Young & Co. Sheffield 1779	
,, ,, 1722		,, ,, 1779	
,, ,, 1735			

SHEFFIELD PLATE MARKS

SHEFFIELD PLATE MARKS

The marks to be found on Sheffield Plate have been treated in two sections. The first section includes all of those marks which contain initials. Where a name is provided in the mark, we have listed it under the initial letter of the SURNAME. Where initials only have been used in the mark and because these do not always relate readily to the maker's actual name, we have entered them under the first intial letter, reading left to right. Where, of the initial letters contained, one of them is obviously dominant, we have listed the mark under the dominating letter.

The second small section on p. 114 includes those marks which are of a pictorial nature. In it are contained those marks that bear neither initials nor names.

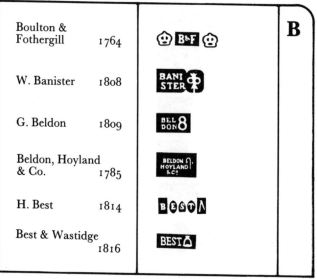

Ashforth Ellis & Co.	1770	
A. Hatfield	1808	
J. Allgood	1812	
G. Ashforth & Co.	1784	
Ashley	1816	
Askew	1828	A SKEW MAKER NOTTINGHAM
E. Allport	1812	

A

Boulton & Fothergill	1764	
W. Banister	1808	
G. Beldon	1809	
Beldon, Hoyland & Co.	1785	
H. Best	1814	
Best & Wastidge	1816	

B

B		
	W BINGLEY	W. Bingley 1787
		Thomas Bishop 1830
		J. Bradshaw 1822
	BRITTAIN WILKIN SON & BROWNILL	Brittain, Wilkinson & Brownhill 1785

C		
		J. Gilbert 1812
		J. Gilbert 1812
		J. Gilbert 1812
	Ches ton	T. Cheston 1809
	CHILD	T. Child 1812
	W COLDWELL.	W. Coldswell 1806
	COPE	C. G. Cope 1817
	CORN &Cº	J. Corn and J. Sheppard 1819
	CRACK NALL	J. Cracknall 1814
	CRESWICKS	T. & J. Creswick 1811

		C
J. F. Causer 1824	CAUSER ♛	

		D
D. Not attributed 1760		
J. Dixon & Sons 1835	D ✱ S	
J. Dixon & Sons 1835	D✱S	
J. Davis 1816	DAVIS J	
Deakin Smith & Co. 1785	DEAKIN SMITH & Cᵒ	
J. Dixon & Sons 1835	Dixon J	
J. Dixon & Sons 1835	G⊗R DIXON'S IMPERIAL	
J. Dixon & Sons 1835	DIXON	
T. Dixon & Co. 1784	DIXON & Cᵒ	
I. Drabble & Co. 1805	I DRABBLE & Cᵒ	
G. B. Dunn 1810	DUNN	

E	ELL ER BY ✦	W. Ellerby	1803
	S·EVANS	S. Evans	1816

F	FOX PROCTOR ♥ PASMORE & C° ✦	T. Fox & Co.	1784
	FREETH ◠	H. Freeth	1816
	C+ K O ◁ HF	H. Freeth	1816
	FROGGATT COLDWELL & LEAN	Frogatt, Coldwell and Lean	1797

G	GA	R. Gainsford	1808
	GH ♀ ♀	G. Harrison	1823
	GH ♀ F	G. Harrison	1823
	GBBS ⊠ ⊠	G. Gibbs	1808
		G. Gibbs	1808
	GARNETT	W. Garnett	1803
	A GOODMAN & Co	Goodman, Gainsforth and Fairbairn	1800

G

E. Goodwin	1795	E GOODWIN
J. Green & Co.	1799	I·GREEN&Cº
J. Green	1807	GREEN
W. Green & Co.	1784	W GREEN &Cº

H

D. & G. Holly	1821	
Henry Atkin	1823	H A
Henry Hall	1829	
Tudor & Leader	1760	T &Cº
Tudor & Leader	1760	
W. Hutton	1839	H & S
W. Hall	1820	HALL
W. Hall	1820	
Joseph Hancock	1755	IOSʰ HANCOCK SHEFFIELD.
M. Hanson	1810	HAN SON
J. Harrison	1809	HARRI SON
T. Harwood	1816	

H		
HILL&Cº	D. Hill & Co.	1806
HINKS	J. Hinks	1812
HIPKISS	J. Hipkiss	1808
Hob day ◇ Hob day	J. Hobday	1829
HOLLAND&Cº	H. Holland & Co. 1784	
DANºHOLY WILKINSON & Cº	Daⁿ Holly, Wilkinson & Co. 1784	
DAN HOLY PARKER & Cº	Dan Holly, Parker & Co.	1804
HOLY Sᴬ C SHEFFIELD	D. & G. Holly	1821
D·HORTON┼	D. Horton	1808
HOR• TON	J. Horton	1809
How- a rd	S. & T. Howard	1809
Hutton 2S	W. Hutton	1807
Hutton 2S Sheffield 2S	W. Hutton	1831
Hutton Ω Hutton Ω	W. Hutton	1837

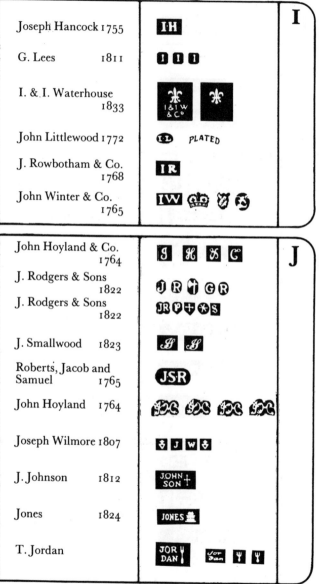

I

Joseph Hancock 1755

G. Lees   1811

I. & I. Waterhouse
       1833

John Littlewood 1772   PLATED

J. Rowbotham & Co.
       1768

John Winter & Co.
       1765

J

John Hoyland & Co.
       1764

J. Rodgers & Sons
       1822

J. Rodgers & Sons
       1822

J. Smallwood   1823

Roberts, Jacob and
Samuel   1765

John Hoyland   1764

Joseph Wilmore 1807

J. Johnson   1812

Jones   1824

T. Jordan

K	KIRKBY FOR·USE	S. Kirkby	1812

L	LAW&SON	J. Law & Son	1807
	R.LAW.	R. Law	1807
	𝕿 TH° LAW 𝕿	Thomas Law	1758
	𝕿 LAW 𝕿	Thomas Law	1758
	THO·LAW & C°	Thomas Law	1758
	A·C·LEA	A. C. Lea	1808
	LEES	G. Lees	1811
	LILLY	John Lilly	1815
	JOSH·LILLY	Joseph Lilly	1816
	LIN WOOD	M. Linwood & Sons	1808
	I·LIN WOOD · I·LIN WOOD	J. Linwood	1807
	I LIN WOOD · I LIN WOOD	J. Linwood	1807
	W·LIN WOOD · W·LIN WOOD	W. Linwood	1807
	I·LOVE & C°	J. Love & Co. and Love, Silverside, Darby & Co. 1785	

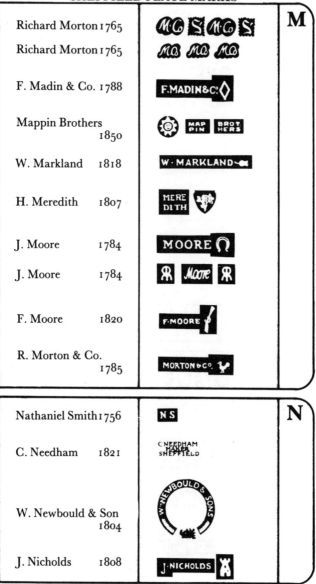

		M
Richard Morton 1765		
Richard Morton 1765		
F. Madin & Co. 1788		
Mappin Brothers 1850		
W. Markland 1818		
H. Meredith 1807		
J. Moore 1784		
J. Moore 1784		
F. Moore 1820		
R. Morton & Co. 1785		

		N
Nathaniel Smith 1756		
C. Needham 1821		
W. Newbould & Son 1804		
J. Nicholds 1808		

O		T. Oldham	1860

P		J. Gilbert	1812
		J. Prime	1839
		J. Prime	1839
		J. Parsons & Co.	1784
		Peak	1807
		Pemberton & Mitchell	1817
		R. Pearson	1811
		J. Prime	1839

R		Robert & Briggs	1860
		Roberts Smith & Co.	1828
		Roberts Cadman & Co.	1785
		J. S. Roberts	1786
		J. Rodgers & Sons	1822

SHEFFIELD PLATE MARKS

J. Rogers 1819	ROGERS	**R**
W. Ryland & Son 1807	RYLAND	

J. Smith & Son 1828	SMI TH	**S**
J. Prime 1839	Pme S Pme	
S. Colmore 1790	S C Colmore Patent	
S. & T. Howard 1809	S H & Cº	
W. Scott 1807		
T. Sansom & Sons 1821	SAN SOM	
R. Silk 1809	S O L K	
J. Shepherd 1817	SHEP. HARD	
T. Small 1812	SMALL	
Smith & Co. 1784	SMITH&Cº	
Smith, Tate, Nicholson and Hoult 1810	SMITH&Cº	
W. Smith 1812	SM ITH	
I. Smith 1821	SMITH	

S		
	JOSEPHUS SMITH	J. Smith 1836
	N. SMITH & Cº	N. Smith & Co. 1784
	STANIFORTH PARKIN & Cº	Staniforth, Parkinson & Co. 1784
	Stot	B. Stot 1811
	SYKES & Cº	Sykes & Co. 1784

T		
	TB S	T. Butts 1807
	THO MAS	S. Thomas 1818
	THOMASON	E. Thomason & Dowler 1807
	MANUFACTURED BY E. THOMASON & C°	E. Thomason & Dowler 1807
	TONKS	Tonks & Co. 1824
	TONKS □	Samuel Tonks 1807
	TUDOR & Cº	Tudor, Leader and Nicholson 1784
	S. TURLEY	S. Turley 1816

J. Turton 1820		**T**
J. Turton 1820		
J. Tyndall 1813		

George Waterhouse & Co. 1842		**W**
W. Briggs 1823		
W. Hutton 1849		
W. Jervis 1789		
Waterhouse & Co. 1807		
Watson, Fenton and Bradbury 1795		
Watson, Pass & Co. (Late J. Watson) 1811		
W. Watson 1833	W WATSON MAKER SHEFFIELD	
W. Hipwood 1809		
J. White and White & Allgood 1811		
Joseph Willmore 1807		

SHEFFIELD PLATE MARKS

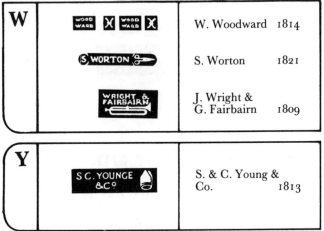

W	
WOOD WARD ✕ WOOD WARD ✕	W. Woodward 1814
S WORTON	S. Worton 1821
WRIGHT & FAIRBAIRN	J. Wright & G. Fairbairn 1809

Y	
S C. YOUNGE &Cº	S. & C. Young & Co. 1813

PICTORIAL MARKS

	M. Boulton & Co. 1784
	Not attributed 1760
	Tudor & Leader 1760
	Fenton Mathews & Co. 1760
	Not attributed 1760

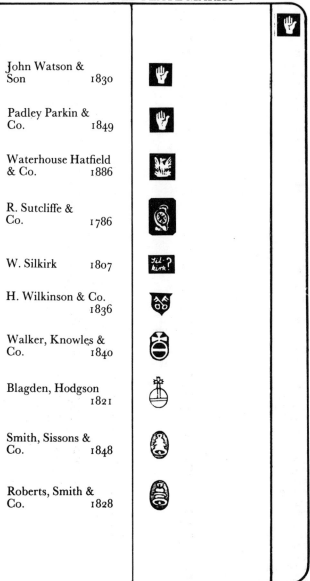

John Watson &
Son   1830

Padley Parkin &
Co.   1849

Waterhouse Hatfield
& Co.   1886

R. Sutcliffe &
Co.   1786

W. Silkirk   1807

H. Wilkinson & Co.
             1836

Walker, Knowles &
Co.   1840

Blagden, Hodgson
             1821

Smith, Sissons &
Co.   1848

Roberts, Smith &
Co.   1828

MAKERS MARKS INDEX

MAKERS MARKS INDEX

MAKERS MARKS INDEX

NOTES

NOTES

NOTES

NOTES

NOTES

NOTES

NOTES

NOTES